shakespeare's

othello

harold bloom

riverhead books
new york

THE BERKLEY PUBLISHING GROUP
Published by the Penguin Group
Penguin Group (USA) Inc.
375 Hudson Street, New York, New York 10014, USA
Penguin Group (Canada), 10 Alcorn Avenue, Toronto, Ontario M4V 3B2, Canada
(a division of Pearson Penguin Canada Inc.)
Penguin Books Ltd., 80 Strand, London WC2R 0RL, England
Penguin Group Ireland, 25 St. Stephen's Green, Dublin 2, Ireland (a division of Penguin Books Ltd.)
Penguin Group (Australia), 250 Camberwell Road, Camberwell, Victoria 3124, Australia
(a division of Pearson Australia Group Pty. Ltd.)
Penguin Books India Pvt. Ltd., 11 Community Centre, Panchsheel Park, New Delhi—110 017, India
Penguin Group (NZ), cnr Airborne and Rosedale Roads, Albany, Auckland 1310, New Zealand
(a division of Pearson New Zealand Ltd.)
Penguin Books (South Africa) (Pty.) Ltd., 24 Sturdee Avenue, Rosebank, Johannesburg 2196, South Africa

Penguin Books Ltd., Registered Offices: 80 Strand, London WC2R 0RL, England

SHAKESPEARE'S OTHELLO

PRINTING HISTORY
First Riverhead trade paperback edition: April 2005
Riverhead trade paperback ISBN: 1-59448-076-1

This book has been catalogued with the Library of Congress.

PRINTED IN THE UNITED STATES OF AMERICA

10   9   8   7   6   5   4   3   2   1

contents

The text of *Othello*, including the synopsis, is that of the old Cambridge Edition (1893), as edited by William Aldis Wright. I am grateful to Brett Foster for indispensable advice upon the editorial revisions I have made in the text.

—Harold Bloom

harold bloom on
othello

The character of Iago . . . belongs to a class of characters common to Shakspeare, and at the same time peculiar to him—namely, that of great intellectual activity, accompanied with a total want of moral principle, and therefore displaying itself at the constant expense of others, and seeking to confound the practical distinctions of right and wrong, by referring them to some overstrained standard of speculative refinement.—Some persons, more nice than wise, have thought the whole of the character of Iago unnatural. Shakspeare, who was quite as good a philosopher as he was a poet, thought otherwise. He knew that the love of power, which is another name for the love of mischief, was natural to man. He would know this as well or better than if it had been demonstrated to him by a logical diagram, merely from seeing children paddle in the dirt, or kill flies for sport. We might ask those who think the character of Iago not natural, why they go to see it performed, but from the interest it excites, the sharper edge which it sets on their curiosity and imagination? Why do we go to see tragedies in general? Why do we always read the accounts in the newspapers of dreadful fires and shocking murders, but for the same reason? Why do so many persons frequent executions and trials, or why do the lower classes almost universally take delight in barbarous sports and cruelty to animals, but because there is a natural tendency in the mind to strong excitement, a desire to have its faculties roused and stimulated to the utmost? Whenever this principle is not under the restraint of humanity, or the sense of moral obligation, there are no excesses to which it will not of itself give rise, without the assistance of any other motive, either of passion or self-interest. Iago is only an extreme instance of the kind; that is, of diseased intellectual activity, with an almost perfect indifference to moral good or evil, or rather with a preference of the latter, because it falls more in with his favourite propensity, gives greater zest to his thoughts, and scope to his actions.—Be it observed, too, (for the sake of those who are for squaring all human actions by the maxims of Rochefoucault), that he is quite or nearly as indifferent to his own fate as to that of others; that he runs all risks for a trifling and doubtful advantage; and is himself the dupe and victim of his ruling passion—an incorrigible love of mischief—an insatiable craving after action of the most difficult and dangerous kind. Our "Ancient" is a philosopher, who fancies that a lie that kills has more point in it than an alliteration or an antithesis; who thinks a fatal experiment on the peace of a family a better thing than watching the palpitations in the heart of a flea in an air-pump; who plots the ruin of his friends as an exercise for his understanding, and stabs men in the dark to prevent *ennui*.

—William Hazlitt

Since it is Othello's tragedy, even if it is Iago's play (not even Hamlet or Edmund seem to compose so much of their dramas), we need to restore some sense of Othello's initial dignity and glory. A bad modern tradition of criticism that goes from T. S. Eliot and F. R. Leavis through current New Historicism has divested the hero of his splendor, in effect doing Iago's work so that, in Othello's words, "Othello's occupation's gone." Since 1919 or so, generals have lost esteem among the elite, though not always among the groundlings. Shakespeare himself subjected chivalric valor to the superb comic critique of Falstaff, who did not leave intact very much of the nostalgia for military prowess. But Falstaff, although he still inhabited a corner of Hamlet's consciousness, is absent from *Othello*.

The clown scarcely comes on stage in *Othello,* though the Fool in *Lear,* the drunken porter at the gate in *Macbeth,* and the fig-and-asp seller in *Antony and Cleopatra* maintain the persistence of tragicomedy in Shakespeare after *Hamlet.* Only *Othello* and *Coriolanus* exclude all laughter, as if to protect two great captains from the Falstaffian perspective. When Othello, doubtless the fastest sword in his profession, wants to stop a street fight, he need only utter the one massive and menacingly monosyllabic line "Keep up your bright swords, for the dew will rust them."

To see Othello in his unfallen splendor, within the play, becomes a little difficult, because he so readily seems to become Iago's dupe. Shakespeare, as before in *Henry IV, Part One,* and directly after in *King Lear,* gives us the responsibility of foregrounding by inference. As the play opens, Iago assures his gull, Roderigo, that he hates Othello, and he states the only true motive for his hatred, which is what Milton's Satan calls "a Sense of Injured Merit." Satan (as Milton did not wish to know) is the legitimate son of Iago, begot by Shakespeare upon Milton's Muse. Iago, long Othello's "ancient" (his ensign, or flag officer, the third-in-command), has been passed over for promotion, and

Cassio has become Othello's lieutenant. No reason is given for Othello's decision; his regard for "honest Iago," bluff veteran of Othello's "big wars," remains undiminished. Indeed, Iago's position as flag officer, vowed to die rather than let Othello's colors be captured in battle, testifies both to Othello's trust and to Iago's former devotion. Paradoxically, that quasi-religious worship of the war god Othello by his true believer Iago can be inferred as the cause of Iago's having been passed over. Iago, as Harold Goddard finely remarked, is always at war; he is a moral pyromaniac setting fire to all of reality. Othello, the skilled professional who maintains the purity of arms by sharply dividing the camp of war from that of peace, would have seen in his brave and zealous ancient someone who could not replace him were he to be killed or wounded. Iago cannot stop fighting, and so cannot be preferred to Cassio, who is relatively inexperienced (a kind of staff officer) but who is courteous and diplomatic and knows the limits of war.

Sound as Othello's military judgment clearly was, he did not know Iago, a very free artist of himself. The catastrophe that foregrounds Shakespeare's play is what I would want to call the Fall of Iago, which sets the paradigm for Satan's Fall in Milton. Milton's God, like Othello, pragmatically demotes his most ardent devotee, and the wounded Satan rebels. Unable to bring down the Supreme Being, Satan ruins Adam and Eve instead, but the subtler Iago can do far better, because his only God is Othello himself, whose fall becomes the appropriate revenge for Iago's evidently sickening loss of being at rejection, with consequences including what may be sexual impotence, and what certainly is a sense of nullity, of no longer being what one was. Iago is Shakespeare's largest study in ontotheological absence, a sense of the void that follows on from Hamlet's, and that directly precedes Edmund's more restricted but even more affectless excursion into the uncanniness of nihilism. Othello was everything to

Iago, because war was everything; passed over, Iago is nothing, and in warring against Othello, his war is against ontology.

Tragic drama is not necessarily metaphysical, but Iago, who says he is nothing if not critical, also is nothing if not metaphysical. His grand boast "I am not what I am" deliberately repeals St. Paul's "By the grace of God I am what I am." With Iago, Shakespeare is enabled to return to the Machiavel, yet now not to another Aaron the Moor or Richard III, both versions of Barabas, Jew of Malta, but to a character light-years beyond Marlowe. The self-delight of Barabas, Aaron, and Richard III in their own villainy is childlike compared with Iago's augmenting pride in his achievement as psychologist, dramatist, and aesthete (the first modern one) as he contemplates the total ruin of the war god Othello, reduced to murderous incoherence. Iago's accomplishment in revenge tragedy far surpasses Hamlet's revision of *The Murder of Gonzago* into *The Mousetrap.* Contemplate Iago's achievement: his unaided genius has limned this night piece, and it was his best. He will die under torture, silently, but he will have left a mutilated reality as his monument.

Auden, in one of his most puzzling critical essays, found in Iago the apotheosis of the practical joker, which I find explicable only by realizing that Auden's Iago was Verdi's (that is, Boito's), just as Auden's Falstaff was operatic, rather than dramatic. One should not try to restrict Iago's genius; he is a great artist, and no joker. Milton's Satan is a failed theologian and a great poet, while Iago shines equally as nihilistic death-of-God theologue and as advanced dramatic poet. Shakespeare endowed only Hamlet, Falstaff, and Rosalind with more wit and intellect than he gave to Iago and Edmund, while in aesthetic sensibility, only Hamlet overgoes Iago. Grant Iago his Ahab-like obsession—Othello is the Moby-Dick who must be harpooned—and Iago's salient quality rather outrageously is his freedom. A great improviser, he works with gusto and mastery of timing, adjusting his plot to openings as they present themselves. If I were a director of *Othello,* I would instruct my Iago to manifest an ever-growing wonder and confidence in the diabolic art. Unlike Barabas and his progeny, Iago is an inventor, an experimenter always willing to try modes heretofore unknown. Auden, in a more inspired moment, saw Iago as a scientist rather than a practical joker. Satan, exploring the untracked Abyss in *Paradise Lost,* is truly in Iago's spirit. Who before Iago, in literature or in life, perfected the arts of disinformation, disorientation, and derangement? All these combine in Iago's grand program of uncreation, as Othello is returned to original chaos, to the Tohu and Bohu from which we came.

Even a brief glance at Shakespeare's source in Cinthio reveals the extent to which Iago is essentially Shakespeare's radical invention, rather than an adaptation of the wicked Ensign in the original story. Cinthio's Ensign falls passionately in love with Desdemona, but wins no favor with her, since she loves the Moor. The unnamed Ensign decides that his failure is due to Desdemona's love for an unnamed Captain (Shakespeare's Cassio), and so he determines to remove this supposed rival, by inducing jealousy in the Moor and then plotting with him to murder both Desdemona and the Captain. In Cinthio's version, the Ensign beats Desdemona to death, while the Moor watches approvingly. It is only afterward, when the Moor repents and desperately misses his wife, that he dismisses the Ensign, who thus is first moved to hatred against his general. Shakespeare transmuted the entire story by giving it, and Iago, a different starting point, the foreground in which Iago has been passed over for promotion. The ontological shock of that rejection is Shakespeare's original invention and is the trauma that truly creates Iago, no mere wicked Ensign but rather a genius of evil who has engendered himself from a great Fall.

Milton's Satan owes so much to Iago that we can be tempted to read the Christian Fall of Adam into Othello's catastrophe, and to find Lucifer's decline into Satan a clue to Iago's inception. But though Shakespeare's Moor has been baptized, *Othello* is no more a Christian drama than *Hamlet* was a doctrinal tragedy of guilt, sin, and pride. Iago playfully invokes a "Divinity of Hell," and yet he is no mere diabolist. He is War Everlasting (as Goddard sensed) and inspires in me the same uncanny awe and fright that Cormac McCarthy's Judge Holden arouses each time I reread *Blood Meridian, Or, The Evening Redness in the West* (1985). The Judge, though based on an historic filibuster who massacred and scalped Indians in the post–Civil War Southwest and in Mexico, is War Incarnate. A reading of his formidable pronunciamentos provides a theology-in-little of Iago's enterprise, and betrays perhaps a touch of Iago's influence upon *Blood Meridian,* an American descendant of the Shakespeare-intoxicated Melville and Faulkner. "War," says the Judge, "is the truest form of divination . . . War is god," because war is the supreme game of will against will. Iago is the genius of will reborn from war's slighting of the will. To have been passed over for Cassio is to have one's will reduced to nullity, and the self's sense of power violated. Victory for the will therefore demands a restoration of power, and power for Iago can only be war's power: to maim, to kill, to humiliate, to destroy the godlike in another, the war god who betrayed his worship and his trust. Cormac McCarthy's Judge Holden is Iago come again when he proclaims war as the game that defines us:

> Wolves cull themselves, man. What other creature could? And is the race of man not more predacious yet? The way of the world is to bloom and flower and die but in the affairs of men there is no waning and the moon of his expression signals the onset of night. His spirit is exhausted at the peak of its achievement. His meridian is at once his darkening and the evening of his day. He loves games? Let him play for stakes.

In Iago, what was the religion of war, when he worshiped Othello as its god, has now become the game of war, to be played everywhere except upon the battlefield. The death of belief becomes the birth of invention, and the passed-over officer becomes the poet of street brawls, stabbings in the dark, disinformation, and above all else, the uncreation of Othello, the sparagmos of the great captain-general so that he can be returned to the original abyss, the chaos that Iago equates with the Moor's African origins. That is not Othello's view of his heritage (or Shakespeare's), but Iago's interpretation wins, or almost wins, since I will argue that Othello's much-maligned suicide speech is something very close to a recovery of dignity and coherence, though not of lost greatness. Iago, forever beyond Othello's understanding, is not beyond ours, because we are more like Iago than we resemble Othello; Iago's views on war, on the will, and on the aesthetics of revenge inaugurate our own pragmatics of understanding the human.

We cannot arrive at a just estimate of Othello if we undervalue Iago, who would be formidable enough to undo most of us if he emerged out of his play into our lives. Othello is a great soul hopelessly outclassed in intellect and drive by Iago. Hamlet, as A. C. Bradley once observed, would have disposed of Iago very readily. In a speech or two, Hamlet would discern Iago for what he was, and then would drive Iago to suicide by lightning parody and mockery. Falstaff and Rosalind would do much the same, Falstaff boisterously and Rosalind gently. Only humor could defend against Iago, which is why Shakespeare excludes all comedy from Othello, except for Iago's saturnine hilarity. Even there, a difference emerges; Barabas and his Shakespearean imitators share their triumphalism with the audience, whereas Iago, at the top of his form, seems to be sending us postcards from the volcano, as remote from us as he is from all his victims. "You come next," something in him implies, and we wince before him. "With all his poetic gift, he has no poetic weakness," Swinburne said of Iago. The prophet of Resentment, Iago presages Smerdyakov, Svidrigailov, and Stavrogin in Dostoevsky, and all the ascetics of the spirit deplored by Nietzsche.

Yet he is so much more than that; among all literary villains, he is by merit raised to a bad eminence that seems unsurpassable. His only near-rival, Edmund, partly repents while dying, in a gesture more enigmatic than Iago's final election of silence. Great gifts of intellect and art alone could not bring Iago to his heroic villainy; he has a negative grace beyond cognition and per-ceptiveness. The public sphere gave Marlowe his Guise in *The Massacre at Paris,* but the Guise is a mere imp of evil when juxta-posed to Iago. The Devil himself—in Milton, Marlowe, Goethe, Dostoevsky, Melville, or any other writer—cannot compete with Iago, whose American descendants range from Hawthorne's Chillingworth and Melville's Claggart through Mark Twain's Mysterious Stranger on to Nathanael West's Shrike and Cormac McCarthy's Judge Holden. Modern literature has not surpassed Iago; he remains the perfect Devil of the West, superb as psychol-ogist, playwright, dramatic critic, and negative theologian. Shaw, jealous of Shakespeare, argued that "the character defies all con-sistency," being at once "a coarse blackguard" and also refined and subtle. Few have agreed with Shaw, and those who question Iago's persuasiveness tend also to find Othello a flawed represen-tation. A. C. Bradley, an admirable critic always, named Falstaff, Hamlet, Iago, and Cleopatra as Shakespeare's "most wonderful" characters. If I could add Rosalind and Macbeth to make a six-fold wonder, then I would agree with Bradley, for these are Shakespeare's grandest inventions, and all of them take human nature to some of its limits, without violating those limits. Fal-staff 's wit, Hamlet's ambivalent yet charismatic intensity, Cleopa-tra's mobility of spirit find their rivals in Macbeth's proleptic imagination, Rosalind's control of all perspectives, and Iago's genius for improvisation. Neither merely coarse nor merely subtle, Iago constantly re-creates his own personality and character: "I am not what I am." Those who question how a twenty-eight-year-old professional soldier could harbor so sublimely negative a genius might just as soon question how the thirty-nine-year-old professional actor, Shakespeare, could imagine so convincing a "demi-devil" (as Othello finally terms Iago). We think that Shakespeare abandoned acting just before he composed *Othello;* he seems to have played his final role in *All's Well That Ends Well.* Is there some link between giving up the player's part and the invention of Iago? Between *All's Well That Ends Well* and *Othello,* Shakespeare wrote *Measure for Measure,* a farewell to stage comedy. *Measure for Measure's* enigmatic Duke Vincentio, as I have observed, seems to have some Iago-like qualities, and may also relate to Shakespeare's release from the burden of performance. Clearly a versatile and competent actor, but never a leading one, Shakespeare perhaps celebrates a new sense of the actor's energies in the improvisations of Vincentio and Iago.

Bradley, in exalting Falstaff, Hamlet, Iago, and Cleopatra, may have been responding to the highly conscious theatricalism that is fused into their roles. Witty in himself, Falstaff provokes wit in others through his performances. Hamlet, analytical tragedian, discourses with everyone he encounters, driving them to self-revelation. Cleopatra is always on stage—living, loving, and dying—and whether she ceases to perform, when alone with Antony, we will never know, because Shakespeare never shows them alone together, save once, and that is very brief. Perhaps Iago, before the Fall of his rejection by Othello, had not yet discovered his own dramatic genius; it seems the largest pragmatic consequence of his Fall, once his sense of nullity has passed through an initial trauma. When we first hear him, at the start of the play, he already indulges his actor's freedom:

O, sir, content you!
I follow him to serve my turn upon him.
We cannot all be masters, nor all masters
Cannot be truly followed. You shall mark
Many a duteous and knee-crooking knave
That, doting on his own obsequious bondage,
Wears out his time much like his master's ass,
For nought but provender, and, when he's old, cashiered.
Whip me such honest knaves! Others there are
Who, trimmed in forms and visages of duty,
Keep yet their hearts attending on themselves
And, throwing but shows of service on their lords,
Do well thrive by them, and, when they have lined their
    coats,
Do themselves homage: these fellows have some soul
And such a one do I profess myself.

[I.i.40–54]

Only the actor, Iago assures us, possesses "some soul"; the rest of us wear our hearts upon our sleeves. Yet this is only the start of a player's career; at this early point, Iago is merely out for mischief, rousing up Brabantio, Desdemona's father, and conjuring up street brawls. He knows that he is exploring a new vocation, but he has little sense as yet of his own genius. Shakespeare, while Iago gathers force, centers instead upon giving us a view of Othello's precarious greatness, and of Desdemona's surpassing human worth. Before turning to the Moor and his bride, I wish further to foreground Iago, who requires quite as much inferential labor as do Hamlet and Falstaff.

Richard III and Edmund have fathers; Shakespeare gives us no antecedents for Iago. We can surmise the ancient's previous relationship to his superb captain. What can we infer of his marriage to Emilia? There is Iago's curious mistake in his first mention of

Cassio: "A fellow almost damned in a fair wife." This seems not to be Shakespeare's error but a token of Iago's obsessive concern with marriage as a damnation, since Bianca is plainly Cassio's whore and not his wife. Emilia, no better than she should be, will be the ironic instrument that undoes Iago's triumphalism, at the cost of her life. As to the relationship between this singular couple, Shakespeare allows us some pungent hints. Early in the play, Iago tells us what neither he nor we believe, not because of any shared regard for Emilia but because Othello is too grand for this:

> And it is thought abroad that 'twixt my sheets
> He's done my office. I know not if 't be true,
> But I for mere suspicion in that kind
> Will do as if for surety.

> [I.iii.386–89]

Later, Iago parenthetically expresses the same "mere suspicion" of Cassio: "For I fear Cassio with my night-cap too." We can surmise that Iago, perhaps made impotent by his fury at being passed over for promotion, is ready to suspect Emilia with every male in the play, while not particularly caring one way or the other. Emilia, comforting Desdemona after Othello's initial rage of jealousy against his blameless wife, sums up her own marriage also:

> 'Tis not a year or two shows us a man.
> They are all but stomachs, and we all but food:
> They eat us hungerly, and when they are full
> They belch us.

> [III.iv.104–7]

That is the erotic vision of *Troilus and Cressida,* carried over into a greater realm, but not a less rancid one, because the world of *Othello* belongs to Iago. It is not persuasive to say that Othello is a normal man and Iago abnormal; Iago is the genius of his time and place, and is all will. His passion for destruction is the only creative passion in the play. Such a judgment is necessarily very somber, but then this is surely Shakespeare's most painful play. *King Lear* and *Macbeth* are even darker, but theirs is the darkness of the negative sublime. The only sublimity in *Othello* is Iago's. Shakespeare's conception of him was so definitive that the revisions made between the Quarto's text and the Folio's enlarge and sharpen our sense primarily of Emilia, and secondly of Othello and Desdemona, but hardly touch Iago. Shakespeare rightly felt no need to revise Iago, already the perfection of malign will and genius for hatred. There can be no question concerning Iago's primacy in the play: he speaks eight soliloquies, Othello only three.

Edmund outthinks and so outplots everyone else in *King Lear,* and yet is destroyed by the recalcitrant endurance of Edgar, who develops from credulous victim into inexorable revenger. Iago, even more totally the master of his play, is at last undone by Emilia, whom Shakespeare revised into a figure of intrepid outrage, willing to die for the sake of the murdered Desdemona's good name. Shakespeare had something of a tragic obsession with the idea of a good name living on after his protagonists' deaths. Hamlet, despite saying that no man can know anything of whatever he leaves behind him, nevertheless exhorts Horatio to survive so as to defend what might become of his prince's wounded name. We will hear Othello trying to recuperate some shred of reputation in his suicidal final speech, upon which critical agreement no longer seems at all possible. If the *Funeral Elegy* for Will Peter indeed was Shakespeare's (I think this probable), then the poet-dramatist in 1612, four years before his own death at fifty-two, was much preoccupied with his own evidently blemished name.

Emilia's heroic victory over Iago is one of Shakespeare's

grandest ironies, and appropriately constitutes the play's most surprising dramatic moment:

> *Emilia.* O God, O heavenly God!
> *Iago.*   Zounds, hold your peace!
> *Emilia.* 'Twill out, 'twill out! I peace?
>   No, I will speak as liberal as the north.
>   Let heaven and men and devils, let them all,
>   All, all cry shame against me, yet I'll speak.
> *Iago.* Be wise, and get you home.
> *Emilia.* I will not.
>   Iago *tries to stab* Emilia.
> *Gratiano.* Fie! Your sword upon a woman?
> *Emilia.* O thou dull Moor, that handkerchief thou speak'st of
>   I found by fortune and did give my husband,
>   For often, with a solemn earnestness—
>   More than indeed belonged to such a trifle—
>   He begged of me to steal't.
> *Iago.*   Villainous whore!
> *Emilia.* She give it to Cassio? No, alas, I found it
>   And I did give't my husband.
> *Iago.*   Filth, thou liest!
> *Emilia.* By heaven, I do not, I do not, gentlemen!
>   O murderous coxcomb, what should such a fool
>   Do with so good a wife?
>   Othello *runs at* Iago. Iago *stabs his wife.*
> *Othello.*   Are there no stones in heaven
>   But what serves for the thunder? Precious villain!
> *Gratiano.* The woman falls, sure he hath killed his wife.
> *Emilia.* Ay, ay; O lay me by my mistress' side.
>   *Exit* Iago.
> *Gratiano.* He's gone, but his wife's killed.
>   [V.ii.216–36]

We are surprised, but Iago is shocked, indeed it is his first reversal since being passed over for Cassio. That Emilia should lose her worldly wisdom, and become as free as the north wind, was the only eventuality that Iago could not foresee. And his failure to encompass his wife's best aspect—her love for and pride in Desdemona—is the one lapse for which he cannot forgive himself. That is the true undersong of the last lines he ever will allow himself to utter, and which are directed as much to us as to Othello or to Cassio:

> *Othello.* Will you, I pray, demand that demi-devil
>   Why he hath thus ensnared my soul and body?
> *Iago.* Demand me nothing. What you know, you know.
>   From this time forth I never will speak word.
>
> [V.ii.298–301]

What is it that we know, beyond what Othello and Cassio know? Shakespeare's superb dramatic irony transcends even that question into the subtler matter of allowing us to know something about Iago that the ancient, despite his genius, is incapable of knowing. Iago is outraged that he could not anticipate, by dramatic imagination, his wife's outrage that Desdemona should be not only murdered but perhaps permanently defamed The aesthete's web has all of war's gamelike magic, but no place in it for Emilia's honest indignation. Where he ought to have been at his most discerning—within his marriage—Iago is blank and blind. The superb psychologist who unseamed Othello, and who deftly manipulated Desdemona, Cassio, Roderigo, and all others, angrily falls into the fate he arranged for his prime victim, the Moor, and becomes another wife murderer. He has, at last, set fire to himself.

2

Since the world is Iago's, I scarcely am done expounding him, and will examine him again in an overview of the play, but only after brooding upon the many enigmas of Othello. Where Shakespeare granted Hamlet, Lear, and Macbeth an almost continuous and preternatural eloquence, he chose instead to give Othello a curiously mixed power of expression, distinct yet divided, and deliberately flawed. Iago's theatricalism is superb, but Othello's is troublesome, brilliantly so. The Moor tells us that he has been a warrior since he was seven, presumably a hyperbole but indicative that he is all too aware his greatness has been hard won. His professional self-awareness is extraordinarily intense; partly this is inevitable, since he is technically a mercenary, a black soldier of fortune who honorably serves the Venetian state. And yet his acute sense of his reputation betrays what may well be an uneasiness, sometimes manifested in the baroque elaborations of his language, satirized by Iago as "a bombast circumstance, / Horribly stuffed with epithets of war."

A military commander who can compare the movement of his mind to the "icy current and compulsive course" of the Pontic (Black) Sea, Othello seems incapable of seeing himself except in grandiose terms. He presents himself as a living legend or walking myth, nobler than any antique Roman. The poet Anthony Hecht thinks that we are meant to recognize "a ludicrous and nervous vanity" in Othello, but Shakespeare's adroit perspectivism evades so single a recognition. Othello has a touch of Shakespeare's Julius Caesar in him; there is an ambiguity in both figures that makes it very difficult to trace the demarcations between their vainglory and their grandeur. If you believe in the war god Caesar (as Antony does) or in the war god Othello (as Iago once did), then you lack the leisure to contemplate the god's failings. But if you are Cassius, or the postlapsarian Iago, then you are at pains to behold the weaknesses that mask as divinity. Othello, like Caesar, is prone to refer to himself in the third person, a somewhat unnerving habit, whether in literature or in life. And yet, again like Julius Caesar, Othello believes his own myth, and to some extent we must also, because there is authentic nobility in the language of his soul. That there is opacity also, we cannot doubt; Othello's tragedy is precisely that Iago should know him better than the Moor knows himself.

Othello is a great commander, who knows war and the limits of war but who knows little else, and cannot know that he does not know. His sense of himself is very large, in that its scale is vast, but he sees himself from afar as it were; up close, he hardly confronts the void at his center. Iago's apprehension of that abyss is sometimes compared to Montaigne's; I sooner would compare it to Hamlet's, because like one element in the infinitely varied prince of Denmark, Iago is well beyond skepticism and has crossed into nihilism. Iago's most brilliant insight is that if *he* was reduced to nothingness by Cassio's preferment, then how much more vulnerable Othello must be, lacking Iago's intellect and game-playing will. Anyone can be pulverized, in Iago's view, and in this drama he is right. There is no one in the play with the irony and wit that alone could hold off Iago: Othello is consciously theatrical but quite humorless, and Desdemona is a miracle of sincerity. The terrible painfulness of *Othello* is that Shakespeare shrewdly omits any counterforce to Iago. In *King Lear,* Edmund also confronts no one with the intellect to withstand him, until he is annihilated by the exquisite irony of having created the nameless avenger who was once his gull, Edgar. First and last, Othello is powerless against Iago; that helplessness is the most harrowing element in the play, except perhaps for Desdemona's double powerlessness, in regard both to Iago and to her husband.

It is important to emphasize the greatness of Othello, despite all his inadequacies of language and of spirit. Shakespeare implicitly celebrates Othello as a giant of mere being, an ontological splendor, and so a natural man self-raised to an authentic if precarious eminence. Even if we doubt the possibility of the purity of arms, Othello plausibly represents that lost ideal. At every point, he is the antithesis of Iago's "I am not what I am," until he begins to come apart under Iago's influence. Manifestly, Desdemona has made a wrong choice in a husband, and yet that choice testifies to Othello's hard-won splendor. These days, when so many academic critics are converted to the recent French fashion of denying the self, some of them happily seize upon Othello as a fit instance. They undervalue how subtle Shakespeare's art can be; Othello indeed may seem to prompt James Calderwood's Lacanian observation:

> Instead of a self-core discoverable at the center of his being, Othello's "I am" seems a kind of internal repertory company, a "we are."

If Othello, at the play's start, or at its close, is only the sum of his self-descriptions, then indeed he could be judged a veritable picnic of souls. But his third-person relation to his own images of self testifies not to a "we are" but to a perpetual romanticism at seeing and describing himself. To some degree, he is a self-enchanter, as well as the enchanter of Desdemona. Othello desperately wants and needs to be the protagonist of a Shakespearean romance, but alas he is the hero-victim of this most painful Shakespearean domestic tragedy of blood. John Jones makes the fine observation that Lear in the Quarto version is a romance figure, but then is revised by Shakespeare into the tragic being of the Folio text. As Iago's destined gull, Othello presented Shakespeare with enormous problems in representation. How are we to believe in the essential heroism, largeness, and loving nature of so catastrophic a protagonist? Since Desdemona is the most admirable image of love in all Shakespeare, how are we to sympathize with her increasingly incoherent destroyer, who renders her the unluckiest of all wives? Romance, literary and human, depends on partial or imperfect knowledge. Perhaps Othello never gets beyond that, even in his final speech, but Shakespeare shrewdly frames the romance of Othello within the tragedy of *Othello,* and thus solves the problem of sympathetic representation.

Othello is not a "poem unlimited," beyond genre, like *Hamlet,* but the romance elements in its three principal figures do make it a very uncommon tragedy. Iago is a triumph because he is in exactly the right play for an ontotheological villain, while the charitable Desdemona is superbly suited to this drama also. Othello cannot quite fit, but then that is his socio-political dilemma, the heroic Moor commanding the armed forces of Venice, sophisticated in its decadence then as now. Shakespeare mingles commercial realism and visionary romance in his portrait of Othello, and the mix necessarily is unsteady, even for this greatest of all makers. Yet we do Othello wrong to offer him the show of violence, whether by unselfing him or by devaluing his goodness. Iago, nothing if not critical, has a keener sense of Othello than most of us now tend to achieve:

> The Moor is of a free and open nature
> That thinks men honest that but seem to be so.

There are not many in Shakespeare, or in life, that are "of a free and open nature": to suppose that we are to find Othello ludicrous or paltry is to mistake the play badly. He is admirable, a tower among men, but soon enough he becomes a broken tower. Shakespeare's own Hector, Ulysses, and Achilles, in his *Troilus and Cressida,* were all complex travesties of their Homeric originals (in George Chapman's version), but Othello is precisely Homeric, as close as Shakespeare desired to come to Chapman's heroes. Within his clear limitations, Othello indeed is "noble": his consciousness, prior to his fall, is firmly controlled, just, and massively dignified, and has its own kind of perfection. Reuben Brower admirably said of Othello that "his heroic simplicity was also heroic blindness. That too is part of the 'ideal' hero, part of Shakespeare's metaphor." The metaphor, no longer quite Homeric, had to extend to the professionalism of a great mercenary soldier and a heroic black in the service of a highly decadent white society. Othello's superb professionalism is at once his extraordinary strength and his tragic freedom to fall. The love between Desdemona and Othello is authentic, yet might have proved catastrophic even in the absence of the daemonic genius of Iago. Nothing in Othello is marriageable: his military career fulfills him completely. Desdemona, persuasively innocent in the highest of senses, falls in love with the pure warrior in Othello, and he falls in love with her love for him, her mirroring of his legendary career. Their romance is his own pre-existent romance; the marriage does not and cannot change him, though it changes his relationship to Venice, in the highly ironic sense of making him more than ever an outsider.

Othello's character has suffered the assaults of T. S. Eliot and F. R. Leavis and their various followers, but fashions in Shakespeare criticism always vanish, and the noble Moor has survived his denigrators. Yet Shakespeare has endowed Othello with the authentic mystery of being a radically flawed hero, an Adam too free to fall. In some respects, Othello is Shakespeare's most wounding representation of male vanity and fear of female sexuality, and so of the male equation that makes the fear of cuckoldry and the fear of mortality into a single dread. Leontes, in *The Winter's Tale,* is partly a study in repressed homosexuality, and thus his virulent jealousy is of another order than Othello's. We wince when Othello, in his closing apologia, speaks of himself as one not easily jealous, and we wonder at his blindness. Still we never doubt his valor, and this makes it even stranger that he at least matches Leontes in jealous madness. Shakespeare's greatest insight into male sexual jealousy is that it is a mask for the fear of being castrated by death. Men imagine that there never can be enough time and space for themselves, and they find in cuckoldry, real or imaginary, the image of their own vanishing, the realization that the world will go on without them.

Othello sees the world as a theater for his professional reputation; this most valiant of soldiers has no fear of literal death-in-battle, which only would enhance his glory. But to be cuckolded by his own wife, and with his subordinate Cassio as the other offender, would be a greater, metaphorical death-in-life, for his reputation would not survive it, particularly in his own view of his mythic renown. Shakespeare is sublimely daemonic, in a mode transcending even Iago's genius, in making Othello's vulnerability exactly consonant with the wound rendered to Iago's self-regard by being passed over for promotion. Iago says, "I am not what I am"; Othello's loss of ontological dignity would be even greater, had Desdemona "betrayed" him (I place the word between quotation marks, because the implicit metaphor involved is a triumph of male vanity). Othello all too self-consciously has risked his hard-won sense of his own being in marrying Desdemona, and he has an accurate foreboding of chaotic engulfment should that risk prove a disaster:

Excellent wretch! Perdition catch my soul
But I do love thee! and when I love thee not
Chaos is come again.

[III.iii.90–92]

An earlier intimation of Othello's uneasiness is one of the play's subtlest touches:

> For know, Iago,
> But that I love the gentle Desdemona
> I would not my unhoused free condition
> Put into circumscription and confine
> For the sea's worth.
>
> [I.ii.24–28]

Othello's psychological complexity has to be reconstructed by the audience from his ruins, as it were, because Shakespeare does not supply us with the full foreground. We are given the hint that but for Desdemona, he never would have married, and indeed he himself describes a courtship in which he was essentially passive:

> This to hear
> Would Desdemona seriously incline,
> But still the house affairs would draw her thence,
> Which ever as she could with haste dispatch
> She'd come again, and with a greedy ear
> Devour up my discourse; which I, observing,
> Took once a pliant hour and found good means
> To draw from her a prayer of earnest heart
> That I would all my pilgrimage dilate,
> Whereof by parcels she had something heard
> But not intentively. I did consent,
> And often did beguile her of her tears
> When I did speak of some distressful stroke
> That my youth suffered. My story being done
> She gave me for my pains a world of kisses.
> She swore in faith 'twas strange, 'twas passing strange,
> 'Twas pitiful, 'twas wondrous pitiful;
> She wished she had not heard it, yet she wished
> That heaven had made her such a man. She thanked me

And bade me, if I had a friend that loved her,
I should but teach him how to tell my story
And that would woo her. Upon this hint I spake:
She loved me for the dangers I had passed
And I loved her that she did pity them.

[I.iii.146–69]

That is rather more than a "hint," and nearly constitutes a boldly direct proposal, on Desdemona's part. With the Venetian competition evidently confined to the likes of Roderigo, Desdemona is willingly seduced by Othello's naïve but powerful romance of the self, provocative of that "world of kisses." The Moor is not only noble; his saga brings "a maiden never bold" (her father's testimony) "to fall in love with what she feared to look on." Desdemona, a High Romantic centuries ahead of her time, yields to the fascination of quest, if *yields* can be an accurate word for so active a surrender. No other match in Shakespeare is so fabulously unlikely, or so tragically inevitable. Even in a Venice and a Cyprus without Iago, how does so improbable a romance domesticate itself? The high point of passion between Othello and Desdemona is their reunion on Cyprus:

Othello. O my fair warrior!
Desdemona.   My dear Othello.
Othello. It gives me wonder great as my content
    To see you here before me. O my soul's joy,
    If after every tempest come such calms
    May the winds blow till they have wakened death,
    And let the labouring bark climb hills of seas,
    Olympus-high, and duck again as low
    As hell's from heaven. If it were now to die
    'Twere now to be most happy, for I fear
    My soul hath her content so absolute

> That not another comfort like to this
> Succeeds in unknown fate.
Desdemona.   The heavens forbid
> But that our loves and comforts should increase
> Even as our days do grow.
Othello.   Amen to that, sweet powers!
> I cannot speak enough of this content,
> It stops me here, it is too much of joy.
> And this, and this the greatest discords be

>   *They kiss.*

> That e'er our hearts shall make.

>   [II.i.180–96]

From such an apotheosis one can only descend, even if the answering chorus were not Iago's aside that he will loosen the strings now so well tuned. Shakespeare (as I have ventured before, following my master, Dr. Johnson) came naturally to comedy and to romance, but violently and ambivalently to tragedy. *Othello* may have been as painful for Shakespeare as he made it for us. Placing the precarious nobility of Othello and the fragile romanticism of Desdemona upon one stage with the sadistic aestheticism of Iago (ancestor of all modern literary critics) was already an outrageous coup of self-wounding on the poet-dramatist's part. I am delighted to revive the now scoffed-at romantic speculation that Shakespeare carries a private affliction, an erotic vastation, into the high tragedies, *Othello* in particular. Shakespeare is, of course, not Lord Byron, scandalously parading before Europe the pageant of his bleeding heart, yet the incredible agony we rightly undergo as we observe Othello murdering Desdemona has a private as well as public intensity informing it. Desdemona's murder is the crossing point between the overflowing cosmos of Hamlet and the cosmological emptiness of Lear and of Macbeth.

3

The play *Hamlet* and the mind of Hamlet verge upon an identity, since everything that happens to the Prince of Denmark already seems to be the prince. We cannot quite say that the mind of Iago and the play *Othello* are one, since his victims have their own greatness. Yet, until Emilia confounds him, the drama's action is Iago's; only the tragedy of their tragedy belongs to Othello and Desdemona. In 1604, an anonymous storyteller reflected upon "Shakespeare's tragedies, where the Comedian rides, when the Tragedian stands on Tip-toe." This wonderful remark was made of Prince Hamlet, who "pleased all," but more subtly illuminates *Othello,* where Shakespeare-as-comedian rides Iago, even as the dramatist stands on tip-toe to extend the limits of his so painful art. We do not know who in Shakespeare's company played Iago against Burbage's Othello, but I wonder if it was not the great clown Robert Armin, who would have played the drunken porter at the gate in *Macbeth,* the Fool in *King Lear,* and the asp bearer in *Antony and Cleopatra.* The dramatic shock in Othello is that we delight in Iago's exuberant triumphalism, even as we dread his villainy's consequences. Marlowe's self-delighting Barabas, echoed by Aaron the Moor and Richard III, seems a cruder Machiavel when we compare him with the refined Iago, who confounds Barabas with aspects of Hamlet, in order to augment his own growing inwardness. With Hamlet, we confront the ever-growing inner self, but Iago has no inner self, only a fecund abyss, precisely like his descendant, Milton's Satan, who in every deep found a lower deep opening wide. Satan's discovery is agonized; Iago's is diabolically joyous. Shakespeare invents in Iago a sublimely sadistic comic poet, an archon of nihilism who delights in returning his war god to an uncreated night. Can you invent Iago without delighting in your invention, even as we delight in our ambivalent reception of Iago?

Iago is not larger than his play; he perfectly fits it, unlike Hamlet, who would be too large even for the most unlimited of plays. I have noted already that Shakespeare made significant revision to what is spoken by Othello, Desdemona, and Emilia (even Roderigo) but not by Iago; it is as though Shakespeare knew he had gotten Iago right the first time round. No villain in all literature rivals Iago as a flawless conception, who requires no improvement. Swinburne was accurate: "the most perfect evildom, the most potent demi-devil," and "a reflection by hell-fire of the figure of Prometheus." A Satanic Prometheus may at first appear too High Romantic, yet the pyromaniac Iago encourages Roderigo to a

> dire yell
> As when by night and negligence the fire
> Is spied in populous cities.
>
> [I.i.74–76]

According to the myth, Prometheus steals fire to free us; Iago steals us, as fresh fodder for the fire. He is an authentic Promethean, however negative, because who can deny that Iago's fire is poetic? The hero-villains of John Webster and Cyril Tourneur are mere names on the page when we contrast them with Iago; they lack Promethean fire. Who else in Shakespeare, except for Hamlet and Falstaff, is so creative as Iago? These three alone can read your soul, and read everyone they encounter. Perhaps Iago is the recompense that the Negative demanded to counterbalance Hamlet, Falstaff, and Rosalind. Great wit, like the highest irony, needs an inner check in order not to burn away everything else: Hamlet's disinterestedness, Falstaff's exuberance, Rosalind's graciousness. Iago is nothing at all, except critical; there can be no inner check when the self is an abyss. Iago has the single affect of sheer gusto, increasingly aroused as he discovers his genius for improvisation.

Since the plot of *Othello* essentially is Iago's plot, improvisation by Iago constitutes the tragedy's heart and center. Hazlitt's review of Edmund Kean's performance as Iago in 1814, from which I have drawn my epigraph for this chapter, remains the finest analysis of Iago's improvisatory genius, and is most superb when it observes that Iago "stabs men in the dark to prevent *ennui*." That prophetic insight advances Iago to the Age of Baudelaire, Nietzsche, and Dostoevsky, an Age that in many respects remains our own. Iago is not a Jacobean Italian malcontent, another descendant of Marlowe's Machiavels. His greatness is that he is out ahead of us, though every newspaper and television newscast brings us accounts of his disciples working on every scale, from individual crimes of sadomasochism to international terrorism and massacre. Iago's followers are everywhere: I have watched, with great interest, many of my former students, undergraduate and graduate, pursue careers of Iagoism, both in and out of the academy. Shakespeare's great male intellectuals (as contrasted to Rosalind and Beatrice, among his women) are only four all together: Falstaff and Hamlet, Iago and Edmund. Of these, Hamlet and Iago are also aesthetes, critical consciousnesses of near-preternatural power. Only in Iago does the aesthete predominate, in close alliance with nihilism and sadism.

I place particular emphasis upon Iago's theatrical and poetic genius, as an appreciation of Iago that I trust will be aesthetic without also being sadomasochistic, since that danger always mingles with any audience's enjoyment of Iago's revelations to us. There is no major figure in Shakespeare with whom we are less likely to identify ourselves, and yet Iago is as beyond vice as he is beyond virtue, a fine recognition of Swinburne's. Robert

B. Heilman, who perhaps undervalued Othello (the hero, not the play), made restitution by warning that there was no single way into Iago: "As the spiritual have-not, Iago is universal, that is, many things at once, and of many times at once." Swinburne, perhaps tinged with his usual sadomasochism in his high regard for Iago, prophesied that Iago's stance in hell would be like that of Farinata, who stands upright in his tomb: "as if of Hell he had a great disdain." There is hardly a circle in Dante's *Inferno* that Iago could not inhabit, so vast is his potential for ill.

By interpreting Iago as a genius for improvising chaos in others, a gift born out of his own ontological devastation by Othello, I am in some danger of giving us Iago as a negative theologian, perhaps too close to the Miltonic Satan whom he influenced. As I have tried to emphasize throughout this book, Shakespeare does not write Christian or religious drama; he is not Calderón or (to invoke lesser poet-playwrights) Paul Claudel or T. S. Eliot. Nor is Shakespeare (or Iago) any kind of a heretic; I am baffled when critics argue as to whether Shakespeare was Protestant or Catholic, since the plays are neither. There are gnostic heretical elements in Iago, as there will be in Edmund and in Macbeth, but Shakespeare was not a gnostic, or a hermeticist, or a Neo-Platonic occultist. In his extraordinary way, he was the most curious and universal of gleaners, possibly even of esoteric spiritualities, yet here too he was primarily an inventor or discoverer. Othello is a Christian, by conversion; Iago's religion is war, war everywhere—in the streets, in the camp, in his own abyss. Total war is a religion, whose best literary theologian I have cited already, Judge Holden in Cormac McCarthy's frightening *Blood Meridian*. The Judge imitates Iago by expounding a theology of the will, whose ultimate expression is war, against everyone. Iago says that he has never found a man who knew how to love himself, which means that self-love is the exercise of the will in murdering others. That is

Iago's self-education in the will, since he does not start out with the clear intention of murder. In the beginning was a sense of having been outraged by a loss of identity, accompanied by the inchoate desire to be revenged upon the god Iago had served.

Shakespeare's finest achievement in *Othello* is Iago's extraordinary mutations, prompted by his acute self-overhearing as he moves through his eight soliloquies, and their supporting asides. From tentative, experimental promptings on to excited discoveries, Iago's course develops into a triumphal march, to be ended only by Emilia's heroic intervention. Much of the theatrical greatness of *Othello* inheres in this triumphalism, in which we unwillingly participate. Properly performed, *Othello* should be a momentary trauma for its audience. *Lear* is equally catastrophic, where Edmund triumphs consistently until the duel with Edgar, but *Lear* is vast, intricate, and varied, and not just in its double plot. In *Othello,* Iago is always at the center of the web, ceaselessly weaving his fiction, and snaring us with dark magic: Only Prospero is comparable, a luminous magus who in part is Shakespeare's answer to Iago.

You can judge Iago to be, in effect, a misreader of Montaigne, as opposed to Hamlet, who makes of Montaigne the mirror of nature. Kenneth Gross shrewdly observes that "Iago is at best a nightmare image of so vigilant and humanizing a pyrrhonism as Montaigne's." Pyrrhonism, or radical skepticism, is transmuted by Hamlet into disinterestedness; Iago turns it into a war against existence, a drive that seeks to argue that there is no reason why anything should be, at all. The exaltation of the will, in Iago, emanates from an ontological lack so great that no human emotion possibly could fill it:

Virtue? A fig! 'tis in ourselves that we are thus, or thus. Our bodies are gardens, to the which our wills are

gardeners. So that if we will plant nettles or sow lettuce, set hyssop and weed up thyme, supply it with one
gender of herbs or distract it with many, either to have
it sterile with idleness or manured with industry—why,
the power and corrigible authority of this lies in our
wills. If the balance of our lives had not one scale of
reason to poise another of sensuality, the blood and
baseness of our natures would conduct us to most preposterous conclusions. But we have reason to cool our
raging motions, our carnal stings, our unbitted lusts;
whereof I take this, that you call love, to be a sect or
scion.

[I.iii.320–33]

"Virtue" here means something like "manly strength," while by
"reason" Iago intends only his own absence of significant emotion. This prose utterance is the poetic center of *Othello,* presaging
Iago's conversion of his leader to a reductive and diseased vision of
sexuality. We cannot doubt that Othello loves Desdemona; Shakespeare also may suggest that Othello is amazingly reluctant to make
love to his wife. As I read the play's text, the marriage is never con-
summated, despite Desdemona's eager desires. Iago derides Othello's "weak function"; that seems more a hint of Iago's impotence
than of Othello's, and yet nothing that the Moorish captain-
general says or does reflects an authentic lust for Desdemona. This
certainly helps explain his murderous rage, once Iago has roused
him to jealousy, and also makes that jealousy more plausible, since
Othello literally does not know whether his wife is a virgin, and is
afraid to find out, one way or the other. I join here the minority
view of Graham Bradshaw, and of only a few others, but this
play, of all Shakespeare's, seems to me the most weakly misread,
possibly because its villain is the greatest master of misprision in
Shakespeare, or in literature. Why did Othello marry anyway, if he

does not sexually desire Desdemona? Iago cannot help us here, and Shakespeare allows us to puzzle the matter out for ourselves, without ever giving us sufficient information to settle the question. But Bradshaw is surely right to say that Othello finally testifies Desdemona died a virgin:

> Now: how dost thou look now? O ill-starred wench,
> Pale as thy smock. When we shall meet at compt
> This look of thine will hurl my soul from heaven
> And fiends will snatch at it. Cold, cold, my girl,
> Even like thy chastity.
>
> [V.ii.270–74]

Unless Othello is merely raving, we at least must believe he means what he says: she died not only faithful to him but "cold . . . Even like thy chastity." It is a little difficult to know just what Shakespeare intends Othello to mean, unless his victim had never become his wife, even for the single night when their sexual union was possible. When Othello vows not to "shed her blood," he means only that he will smother her to death, but the frightening irony is there as well: neither he nor Cassio nor anyone else has ever ended her virginity. Bradshaw finds in this a "ghastly tragicomic parody of an erotic death," and that is appropriate for Iago's theatrical achievement.

I want to shift the emphasis from Bradshaw's in order to question a matter upon which Iago had little influence: Why was Othello reluctant, from the start, to consummate the marriage? When, in Act I, Scene iii, the Duke of Venice accepts the love match of Othello and Desdemona, and then orders Othello to Cyprus, to lead its defense against an expected Turkish invasion, the Moor asks only that his wife be housed with comfort and dignity during his absence. It is the ardent Desdemona who requests that she accompany her husband:

So that, dear lords, if I be left behind,
A moth of peace, and he go to war,
The rites for which I love him are bereft me,
And I a heavy interim shall support
By his dear absence. Let me go with him.

[I.iii.256–60]

Presumably by "rites" Desdemona means consummation, rather than battle, and though Othello seconds her, he rather gratuitously insists that desire for her is not exactly hot in him:

Let her have your voice.
Vouch with me, heaven, I therefore beg it not
To please the palate of my appetite,
Nor to comply with heat, the young affects
In me defunct, and proper satisfaction,
But to be free and bounteous to her mind.
And heaven defend your good souls that you think
I will your serious and great business scant
When she is with me. No, when light-winged toys
Of feathered Cupid seel with wanton dullness
My speculative and officed instrument,
That my disports corrupt and taint my business,
Let housewives make a skillet of my helm
And all indign and base adversities
Make head against my estimation.

[I.iii.261–75]

These lines, hardly Othello at his most eloquent, exceed the measure that decorum requires, and do not favor Desdemona. He protests much too much, and hardly betters the case when he urges her off the stage with him:

Come, Desdemona, I have but an hour
Of love, of worldly matter and direction
To spend with thee. We must obey the time.

[I.iii.299–301]

If that "hour" is literal, then "love" will be lucky to get twenty minutes of this overbusy general's time. Even with the Turks impending, the state would surely have allowed its chief military officer an extra hour or two for initially embracing his wife. When he arrives on Cyprus, where Desdemona has preceded him, Othello tells us: "Our wars are done, the Turks are drowned." That would seem to provide ample time for the deferred matter of making love to his wife, particularly since public feasting is now decreed. Perhaps it is more proper to wait for evening, and so Othello bids Cassio command the watch, and duly says to Desdemona: "Come, my dear love, / The purchase made, the fruits are to ensue: / That profit's yet to come 'tween me and you," and exits with her. Iago works up a drunken riot, involving Cassio, Roderigo, and Montano, governor of Cyprus, in which Cassio wounds Montano. Othello, aroused by a tolling bell, enters with Desdemona following soon afterward. We are not told whether there has been time enough for their "rites," but Othello summons her back to bed, while also announcing that he himself will supervise the dressing of Montano's wounds. Which had priority, we do not precisely know, but evidently the general preferred his self-imposed obligation toward the governor to his marital obligation.

Iago's first insinuations of Desdemona's supposed relationship with Cassio would have no effect if Othello knew her to have been a virgin. It is because he does not know that Othello is so vulnerable. "Why did I marry!" he exclaims, and then points to his cuckold's horns when he tells Desdemona: "I have a pain upon my forehead, here," which his poor innocent of a wife attributes to his all-night care of the governor: "Why, that's with watching," and tries to bind it hard with the fatal handkerchief, pushed away by him, and so it falls in Emilia's way. By then, Othello is already Iago's, and is incapable of resolving his doubts through the only sensible course of finally bringing himself to bed Desdemona.

This is a bewildering labyrinth for the audience, and frequently is not overtly addressed by directors of *Othello*, who leave us doubtful of their interpretations, or perhaps they are not even aware of the difficulty that requires interpretation. Shakespeare was capable of carelessness, but not upon so crucial a point, for the entire tragedy turns upon it. Desdemona and Othello, alas, scarcely know each other, and sexually do not know each other at all. Shakespeare's audacious suggestion is that Othello was too frightened or diffident to seize upon the opportunity of the first night in Cyprus, but evaded and delayed the ordeal by devoting himself to the wounded Montano. The further suggestion is that Iago, understanding Othello, fomented the drunken altercation in order to distract his general from consummation, for otherwise Iago's manipulations would have been without consequence. That credits Iago with extraordinary insight into Othello, but no one should be surprised at such an evaluation. We can wonder why Shakespeare did not make all this clearer, except that we need to remember his contemporary audience was far superior to us in comprehending through the ear. They knew how to listen; most of us do not, in our overvisual culture. Shakespeare doubtless would not have agreed with Blake that what could be made explicit to the idiot was not worth his care, but he had learned from Chaucer, in particular, how to be appropriately sly.

Before turning at last to Iago's triumphalism, I feel obliged to answer my own question: Why did Othello marry when his love for Desdemona was only a secondary response to her primary passion for him? This prelude to tragedy seems plausibly compounded of her ignorance—she is still only a child, rather like Juliet—and his confusion. Othello tells us that he had been nine consecutive months in Venice, away from the battlefield and the camp, and thus he was not himself. Fully engaged in his occupation, he would have been immune to Desdemona's charmed condition and to her generous passion for his living legend. Their shared idealism is also their mutual illusion: the idealism is beautiful, but the illusion would have been dissolved even if Othello had not passed over Iago for promotion and so still had Iago's loving worship, rather than the ancient's vengeful hatred. The fallen Iago will teach Othello that the general's failure to know Desdemona, sexually and otherwise, was because Othello did not want to know. Bradshaw brilliantly observes that Iago's genius "is to persuade others that something they had not thought was something they had not *wanted* to think." Iago, having been thrown into a cosmological emptiness, discovers that what he had worshiped as Othello's warlike fullness of being was in part another emptiness, and Iago's triumph is to expand that part into very nearly the whole of Othello.

4

Iago's terrible greatness (what else can we term it?) is also Shakespeare's triumph over Christopher Marlowe, whose Barabas, Jew of Malta, had influenced the young Shakespeare so fiercely. We can observe that Iago transcends Barabas, just as Prospero is beyond Marlowe's Dr. Faustus. One trace of Barabas abides in Iago, though transmogrified by Shakespeare's more glorious villain: self-delight. Exuberance or gusto, the joy of being Sir John Falstaff, is parodied in Iago's negative celebrations, and yet to considerable purpose. Emptied out of significant being, Iago mounts out of his sense of injured merit in his new pride of attainments: dramatist, psychologist, aesthetic critic, diabolic analyst, countertherapist. His uncreation of his captain-general, the return of the magnificent Othello to an original chaos, remains the supreme negation in the history of Western literature, far surpassing the labors of his Dostoevskian disciples, Svidrigailov and Stavrogin, and of his American pupils, Claggart in Melville's *Billy Budd* and Shrike in Nathanael West's *Miss Lonelyhearts.* The only near-rivals to Iago are also his students, Milton's Satan and Cormac McCarthy's Judge in *Blood Meridian.* Compared with Iago, Satan is hampered by having to work on too cosmic a scale: all of nature goes down with Adam and Eve. McCarthy's Judge, the only character in modern fiction who genuinely frightens me, is too much bloodier than Iago to sustain the comparison. Iago stabs a man or two in the dark; the Judge scalps Indians and Mexicans by the hundreds. By working in so close to his prime victim, Iago becomes the Devil-as-matador, and his own best aficionado, since he is nothing if not critical. The only first-rate Iago I have ever seen was Bob Hoskins, who surmounted his director's flaws in Jonathan Miller's BBC television *Othello* of 1981, where Anthony Hopkins as the Moor sank without a trace by being faithful to Miller's Leavisite (or Eliotic) instructions. Hoskins, always best as a gangster, caught many of the accents of Iago's underworld pride in his own preternatural wiliness, and at moments showed what a negative beatification might be, in the pleasure of undoing one's superior at organized violence. Perhaps Hoskins's Iago was a shade more Marlovian than Shakespearean, almost as though Hoskins (or Miller) had *The Jew of Malta* partly in mind, whereas Iago is refined beyond that farcical an intensity.

Triumphalism is Iago's most chilling yet engaging mode; his great soliloquies and asides march to an intellectual music matched in Shakespeare only by aspects of Hamlet, and by a few rare moments when Edmund descends to self-celebration. Iago's inwardness, which sometimes echoes Hamlet's, enhances his repellent fascination for us: How can a sensible emptiness be so labyrinthine? To trace the phases of Iago's entrapment of Othello should answer that question, at least in part. But I pause here to deny that Iago represents something crucial in Othello, an assertion made by many interpreters, the most convincing of whom is Edward Snow. In a reading too reliant upon the Freudian psychic mythology, Snow finds in Iago the overt spirit that is buried in Othello: a universal male horror of female sexuality, and so a hatred of women.

The Age of Freud wanes, and joins itself now, in many, to the Age of Resentment. That all men fear and hate women and sexuality is neither Freudian nor true, though an aversion to otherness is frequent enough, in women as in men. Shakespeare's lovers, men and women alike, are very various; Othello unfortunately is not one of the sanest among them. Stephen Greenblatt suggests that Othello's conversion to Christianity has augmented the Moor's tendency to sexual disgust, a plausible reading of the play's foreground. Iago seems to see this, even as he intuits Othello's reluctance to consummate the marriage, but even that does not mean Iago is an inward component of Othello's psyche, from the start. Nothing can exceed Iago's power of contamination once he truly begins his campaign, and so it is truer to say that Othello comes to represent Iago than to suggest we ought to see Iago as a component of Othello.

Shakespeare's art, as manifested in Iago's ruination of Othello, is in some ways too subtle for criticism to paraphrase. Iago suggests Desdemona's infidelity by at first not suggesting it, hovering near and around it:

Iago.   I do beseech you,
    Though I perchance am vicious in my guess—

As I confess it is my nature's plague
To spy into abuses, and of my jealousy
Shape faults that are not—that your wisdom
From one that so imperfectly conceits
Would take no notice, nor build yourself a trouble
Out of his scattering and unsure observance:
It were not for your quiet nor your good
Nor for my manhood, honesty and wisdom
To let you know my thoughts.

Othello.   Zounds! What dost thou mean?

Iago. Good name in man and woman, dear my lord,
Is the immediate jewel of their souls:
Who steals my purse steals trash—'tis something-
    nothing,
'Twas mine, 'tis his, and has been slave to thousands—
But he that filches from me my good name
Robs me of that which not enriches him
And makes me poor indeed.

Othello.   By heaven, I'll know thy thoughts!

Iago. You cannot, if my heart were in your hand,
Nor shall not whilst 'tis in my custody.

Othello. Ha!

Iago.   O, beware, my lord, of jealousy!
It is the green-eyed monster, which doth mock
The meat it feeds on. That cuckold lives in bliss
Who, certain of his fate, loves not his wronger,
But O, what damned minutes tells he o'er
Who dotes yet doubts, suspects yet strongly loves!

Othello. O misery!

[III.iii.147–73]

This would be outrageous if its interplay between Iago and
Othello were not so persuasive. Iago manipulates Othello by

exploiting what the Moor shares with the jealous God of the Jews, Christians, and Muslims, a barely repressed vulnerability to betrayal. Yahweh and Othello alike are vulnerable because they have risked extending themselves, Yahweh to the Jews and Othello to Desdemona. Iago, whose motto is "I am not what I am," will triumph by tracking this negativity to Othello, until Othello quite forgets he is a man and becomes jealousy incarnate, a parody of the God of vengeance. We underestimate Iago when we consider him only as a dramatist of the self and a psychologist of genius; his greatest power is as a negative ontotheologian, a diabolical prophet who has a vocation for destruction. He is not the Christian devil or a parody thereof, but rather a free artist of himself, uniquely equipped, by experience and genius, to entrap spirits greater than his own in a bondage founded upon their inner flaws. In a play that held a genius opposed to his own—a Hamlet or a Falstaff—he would be only a frustrated malcontent. Given a world only of gulls and victims—Othello, Desdemona, Cassio, Roderigo, even Emilia until outrage turns her—Iago scarcely needs to exercise the full range of powers that he keeps discovering. A fire is always raging within him, and the hypocrisy that represses his satirical intensity in his dealings with others evidently costs him considerable suffering.

That must be why he experiences such relief, even ecstasy, in his extraordinary soliloquies and asides, where he applauds his own performance. Though he rhetorically invokes a "divinity of hell," neither he nor we have any reason to believe that any demon is listening to him. Though married, and an esteemed flag officer, with a reputation for "honesty," Iago is as solitary a figure as Edmund, or as Macbeth after Lady Macbeth goes mad. Pleasure, for Iago, is purely sadomasochistic; pleasure, for Othello, consists in the rightful consciousness of command. Othello loves Desdemona, yet primarily as a response to her love for his triumphal consciousness. Passed over, and so nullified, Iago determines to convert his own sadomasochism into a countertriumphalism, one that will commandeer his commander, and then transform the god of his earlier worship into a degradation of godhood. The chaos that Othello rightly feared if he ceased to love Desdemona has been Iago's natural element since Cassio's promotion. From that chaos, Iago rises as a new Demiurge, a master of uncreation.

In proposing an ontotheological Iago, I build upon A. C. Bradley's emphasis on the passed-over ancient's "resentment," and add to Bradley the idea that resentment can become the only mode of freedom for such great negations as Iago's Dostoevskian disciples, Svidrigailov and Stavrogin. They may seem insane compared with Iago, but they inherited his weird lucidity, and his economics of the will. René Girard, a theoretician of envy and scapegoating, feels compelled to take Iago at his word, and so sees Iago as being sexually jealous of Othello. This is to be yet again entrapped by Iago, and adds an unnecessary irony to Girard's reduction of all Shakespeare to "a theater of envy." Tolstoy, who fiercely resented Shakespeare, complained of Iago, "There are many motives, but they are all vague." To feel betrayed by a god, be he Mars or Yahweh, and to desire restitution for one's wounded self-regard, to me seems the most precise of any villain's motives: return the god to the abyss into which one has been thrown. Tolstoy's odd, rationalist Christianity could not reimagine Iago's negative Christianity.

Iago is one of Shakespeare's most dazzling performers, equal to Edmund and Macbeth and coming only a little short of Rosalind and Cleopatra, Hamlet and Falstaff, superb charismatics. Negative charisma is an odd endowment; Iago represents it uniquely in Shakespeare, and most literary incarnations of it since owe much to Iago. Edmund, in spite of his own nature, has the element of Don Juan in him, the detachment and freedom from hypocrisy that is fatal for those grand hypocrites, Goneril and Regan. Macbeth, whose prophetic imagination has a universal force, excites our sympathies, however bloody his actions. Iago's appeal to us is the power of the negative, which is all of him and only a part of Hamlet. We all have our gods, whom we worship, and by whom we cannot accept rejection. The Sonnets turn upon a painful rejection, of the poet by the young nobleman, a rejection that is more than erotic, and that seems to figure in Falstaff's public disgrace at Hal's coronation. Foregrounding *Othello* requires that we imagine Iago's humiliation at the election of Cassio, so that we hear the full reverberation of

> Though I do hate him as I do hell-pains,
> Yet for necessity of present life
> I must show out a flag and sign of love,
> Which is indeed but sign.
>
> [I.i. 152–55]

The ensign, or ancient, who would have died faithfully to preserve Othello's colors on the battlefield, expresses his repudiation of his former religion, in lines absolutely central to the play. Love of the war god is now but a sign, even though revenge is as yet more an aspiration than a project. The god of war, grand as Othello may be, is a somewhat less formidable figure than the God of the Jews, Christians, and Muslims, but by a superb ontological instinct, Iago associates the jealousy of one god with that of the other:

> I will in Cassio's lodging lose this napkin
> And let him find it. Trifles light as air
> Are to the jealous confirmations strong
> As proofs of holy writ. This may do something.
> The Moor already changes with my poison:
> Dangerous conceits are in their natures poisons
> Which at the first are scarce found to distaste

But with a little art upon the blood
Burn like the mines of sulphur. I did say so.
                    Enter Othello

[III.iii.324–32]

The simile works equally well the other way round: proofs of
Holy Writ are, to the jealous God, strong confirmations, but the
airiest trifles can provoke the Yahweh who in Numbers leads the
Israelites through the wilderness. Othello goes mad, and so does
Yahweh in Numbers. Iago's marvelous pride in his "I did say so"
leads on to a critical music new even to Shakespeare, one which
will engender the aestheticism of John Keats and Walter Pater.
The now obsessed Othello stumbles upon the stage, to be greeted
by Iago's most gorgeous outburst of triumphalism:

Look where he comes. Not poppy nor mandragora
Nor all the drowsy syrups of the world
Shall ever medicine thee to that sweet sleep
Which thou owedst yesterday.

[III.iii.333–36]

If this were only sadistic exultation, we would not receive so
immortal a wound from it; masochistic nostalgia mingles with the
satisfaction of uncreation, as Iago salutes both his own achievement and the consciousness that Othello never will enjoy again.
Shakespeare's Iago-like subtle art is at its highest, as we come to
understand that Othello *does not know* precisely because he has not
known his wife. Whatever his earlier reluctance to consummate
marriage may have been, he now realizes he is incapable of it, and
so cannot attain to the truth about Desdemona and Cassio:

I had been happy if the general camp,
Pioneers and all, had tasted her sweet body,

So I had nothing known. O now for ever
Farewell the tranquil mind, farewell content!
Farewell the plumed troops and the big wars
That makes ambition virtue! O farewell,
Farewell the neighing steed and the shrill trump,
The spirit-stirring drum, th'ear-piercing fife,
The royal banner, and all quality,
Pride, pomp and circumstance of glorious war!
And, O you mortal engines whose rude throats
Th'immortal Jove's dread clamours counterfeit,
Farewell: Othello's occupation's gone.

[III.iii.348–60]

This Hemingwayesque farewell to the big wars has precisely
Hemingway's blend of masculine posturing and barely concealed
fear of impotence. There has been no time since the wedding,
whether in Venice or on Cyprus, for Desdemona and Cassio to
have made love, but Cassio had been the go-between between
Othello and Desdemona in the play's foregrounding. Othello's
farewell here essentially is to any possibility of consummation;
the lost music of military glory has an undersong in which the
martial engines signify more than cannons alone. If Othello's
occupation is gone, then so is his manhood, and with it departs
also the pride, pomp, and circumstance that compelled Desdemona's passion for him, the "circumstance" being more than
pageantry. Chaos comes again, even as Othello's ontological
identity vanishes, in Iago's sweetest revenge, marked by the villain's sublime rhetorical question: "Is't possible? my lord?" What
follows is the decisive moment of the play, in which Iago realizes,
for the first time, that Desdemona must be murdered by Othello:

Othello. Villain, be sure thou prove my love a whore,
    Be sure of it, give me the ocular proof,

Or by the worth of man's eternal soul

Catching hold of him.

Thou hadst been better have been born a dog

Than answer my waked wrath!

Iago.   Is't come to this?

Othello. Make me to see't, or at the least so prove it

That the probation bear no hinge nor loop

To hang a doubt on, or woe upon thy life!

Iago. My noble lord—

Othello. If thou dost slander her and torture me

Never pray more, abandon all remorse;

On horror's head horrors accumulate,

Do deeds to make heaven weep, all earth amazed,

For nothing canst thou to damnation add

Greater than that!

[III.iii.362–76]

Iago's improvisations, until now, had as their purpose the destruction of Othello's identity, fit recompense for Iago's vastation. Suddenly, Iago confronts a grave threat that is also an opportunity: either he or Desdemona must die, with the consequences of her death to crown the undoing of Othello. How can Othello's desire for "the ocular proof" be satisfied?

Iago. And may—but how? how satisfied, my lord?

Would you, the supervisor, grossly gape on?

Behold her topped?

Othello.   Death and damnation! O!

Iago. It were a tedious difficulty, I think,

To bring them to that prospect. Damn them then

If ever mortal eyes do see them bolster

More than their own. What then? how then?

What shall I say? where's satisfaction?

It is impossible you should see this
Were they as prime as goats, as hot as monkeys,
As salt as wolves in pride, as fools as gross
As ignorance made drunk. But yet, I say,
If imputation and strong circumstances
Which lead directly to the door of truth
Will give you satisfaction, you might have't.

[III.iii.397–411]

The only ocular proof possible is what Othello will not essay, as Iago well understands, since the Moor will not try his wife's virginity. Shakespeare shows us jealousy in men as centering upon both visual and temporal obsessions, because of the male fear that there will not be enough time and space for him. Iago plays powerfully upon Othello's now monumental aversion from the only door of truth that could give satisfaction, the entrance into Desdemona. Psychological mastery cannot surpass Iago's control of Othello, when the ensign chooses precisely this moment to introduce "a handkerchief, / I am sure it was your wife's, did I today / See Cassio wipe his beard with." Dramatic mastery cannot exceed Iago's exploitation of Othello's stage gesture of kneeling to swear revenge:

Othello. Even so my bloody thoughts with violent pace
    Shall ne'er look back, ne'er ebb to humble love
    Till that a capable and wide revenge
    Swallow them up. Now by yond marble heaven
    In the due reverence of a sacred vow
    I here engage my words.
Iago.   Do not rise yet.

                                        Iago kneels.

    Witness, you ever-burning lights above,
    You elements that clip us round about,

Witness that here Iago doth give up
The execution of his wit, hands, heart,
To wronged Othello's service. Let him command
And to obey shall be in me remorse
What bloody business ever.

Othello.   I greet thy love
Not with vain thanks but with acceptance bounteous,
And will upon the instant put thee to't.
Within these three days let me hear thee say
That Cassio's not alive.

Iago.   My friend is dead.
'Tis done—at your request. But let her live.

Othello. Damn her, lewd minx: O damn her, damn her!
Come, go with me apart; I will withdraw
To furnish me with some swift means of death
For the fair devil. Now art thou my lieutenant.

Iago. I am your own for ever.

                                        [III.iii.460–82]

It is spectacular theater, with Iago as director: "Do not rise yet." And it is also a countertheology, transcending any Faustian bargain with the Devil, since the stars and the elements serve as witnesses to a murderous pact, which culminates in the reversal of the passing over of Iago in the play's foreground. "Now art thou my lieutenant" means something very different from what Othello can understand, while "I am your own for ever" seals Othello's starry and elemental fate. What remains is only the way down and out, for everyone involved.

5

Shakespeare creates a terrible pathos for us by not showing Desdemona in her full nature and splendor until we know that she is
doomed. Dr. Johnson found the death of Cordelia intolerable;
the death of Desdemona, in my experience as a reader and theater-
goer, is even more unendurable. Shakespeare stages the scene as
a sacrifice, as grimly countertheological as are Iago's passed-over
nihilism and Othello's "godlike" jealousy. Though Desdemona in
her anguish declares she is a Christian, she does not die a martyr
to that faith but becomes only another victim of what could be
called the religion of Moloch, since she is a sacrifice to the war
god whom Iago once worshiped, the Othello he has reduced to
incoherence. "Othello's occupation's gone"; the shattered relic of
Othello murders in the name of that occupation, for he knows no
other, and is the walking ghost of what he was.

Millicent Bell recently has argued that Othello's is an epistemo-
logical tragedy, but only Iago has intellect enough to sustain such a
notion, and Iago is not much interested in how he knows what
he thinks he knows. *Othello,* as much as *King Lear* and *Macbeth,* is
a vision of radical evil; *Hamlet* is Shakespeare's tragedy of an intellectual. Though Shakespeare never would commit himself to
specifically Christian terms, he approached a kind of gnostic or
heretic tragedy in *Macbeth,* as I will attempt to show. Othello has
no transcendental aspect, perhaps because the religion of war does
not allow for any. Iago, who makes a new covenant with Othello
when they kneel together, had lived and fought in what he took
to be an old covenant with his general, until Cassio was preferred
to him. A devout adherent to the fire of battle, his sense of merit
injured by his god, has degraded that god into "an honourable
murderer," Othello's oxymoronic, final vision of his role. Can such
degradation allow the dignity required for a tragic protagonist?

A. C. Bradley rated *Othello* below *Hamlet, Lear,* and *Macbeth* primarily because it gives us no sense of universal powers impinging upon the limits of the human. I think those powers hover in *Othello,* but they manifest themselves only in the gap that divides the earlier, foregrounded relationship between Iago and Othello from the process of ruination that we observe between them. Iago is so formidable a figure because he has uncanny abilities, endowments only available to a true believer whose trust has transmuted into nihilism. Cain, rejected by Yahweh in favor of Abel, is as much the father of Iago as Iago is the precursor of Milton's Satan. Iago murders Roderigo and maims Cassio; it is as inconceivable to Iago as to us that Iago seeks to knife Othello. If you have been rejected by your god, then you attack him spiritually or metaphysically, not merely physically. Iago's greatest triumph is that the lapsed Othello sacrifices Desdemona in the name of the war god Othello, the solitary warrior with whom unwisely she has fallen in love. That may be why Desdemona offers no resistance, and makes so relatively unspirited a defense, first of her virtue and then of her life. Her victimization is all the more complete, and our own horror at it thereby is augmented.

Though criticism frequently has blinded itself to this, Shakespeare had no affection for war, or for violence organized or unorganized. His great killing machines come to sorrowful ends: Othello, Macbeth, Antony, Coriolanus. His favorite warrior is Sir John Falstaff, whose motto is: "Give me life!" Othello's motto could be "Give me honor," which sanctions slaughtering a wife he hasn't known, supposedly not "in hate, but all in honour." Dreadfully flawed, even vacuous at the center as Othello is, he still is meant to be the best instance available of a professional mercenary. What Iago once worshiped was real enough, but more vulnerable even than Iago suspected. Shakespeare subtly intimates that Othello's prior nobility and his later incoherent brutality are two faces of the war god, but it remains the same god. Othello's occupation's gone partly because he married at all. Pent-up resentment, and not repressed lust, animates Othello as he avenges his lost autonomy in the name of his honor. Iago's truest triumph comes when Othello loses his sense of war's limits, and joins Iago's incessant campaign against *being*. "I am not what I am," Iago's credo, becomes Othello's implicit cry. The rapidity and totality of Othello's descent seems at once the play's one weakness and its most persuasive strength, as persuasive as Iago.

Desdemona dies so piteously that Shakespeare risks alienating us forever from Othello:

> *Desdemona.* O, banish me, my lord, but kill me not!
> *Othello.* Down, strumpet!
> *Desdemona.* Kill me tomorrow, let me live tonight!
> *Othello.* Nay, if you strive—
> *Desdemona.* But half an hour!
> *Othello.*   Being done, there is no pause—
> *Desdemona.* But while I say one prayer!
> *Othello.* It is too late.
>
> [V.ii.77–82]

Rather operatically, Shakespeare gives Desdemona a dying breath that attempts to exonerate Othello, which would indeed strain credulity if she were not, as Alvin Kernan wonderfully put it, "Shakespeare's word for love." We are made to believe that this was at once the most natural of young women, and also so loyal to her murderer that her exemplary last words sound almost ironic, given Othello's degradation: "Commend me to my kind lord—O, farewell!" It seems too much more for us to bear that Othello should refuse her final act of love: "She's like a liar gone to burning hell: / 'Twas I that killed her." The influential modern assaults upon Othello by T. S. Eliot and F. R. Leavis take their plausibility (such as it is) from Shakespeare's heaping up of Othello's brutality, stupidity, and unmitigated guilt. But Shakespeare allows Othello a great if partial recovery, in an astonishing final speech:

> Soft you, a word or two before you go.
> I have done the state some service, and they know't:
> No more of that. I pray you, in your letters,
> When you shall these unlucky deeds relate,
> Speak of me as I am. Nothing extenuate,
> Nor set down aught in malice. Then must you speak
> Of one that loved not wisely, but too well;
> Of one not easily jealous, but, being wrought,
> Perplexed in the extreme; of one whose hand,
> Like the base Judean, threw a pearl away
> Richer than all his tribe; of one whose subdued eyes,
> Albeit unused to the melting mood,
> Drops tears as fast as the Arabian trees
> Their medicinable gum. Set you down this,
> And say besides that in Aleppo once,
> Where a malignant and a turbaned Turk
> Beat a Venetian and traduced the state,
> I took by th' throat the circumcised dog
> And smote him—thus! *He stabs himself.*
>
> [V.ii.336–54]

This famous and problematic outburst rarely provokes any critic to agree with any other, yet the Eliot-Leavis interpretation, which holds that Othello essentially is "cheering himself up," cannot be right. The Moor remains as divided a character as Shakespeare ever created; we need give no credence to the absurd blindness of "loved not wisely, but too well," or the outrageous self-deception of "one not easily jealous." Yet we are moved by the truth of "perplexed in the extreme," and by the invocation of Herod, "the base Judean" who murdered his Maccabean wife,

Mariamme, whom he loved. The association of Othello with Herod the Great is the more shocking for being Othello's own judgment upon himself, and is followed by the Moor's tears, and by his fine image of weeping trees. Nor should a fair critic fail to be impressed by Othello's verdict upon himself: that he has become an enemy of Venice, and as such must be slain. His suicide has nothing Roman in it: Othello passes sentence upon himself, and performs the execution. We need to ask what Venice would have done with Othello, had he allowed himself to survive. I venture that he seeks to forestall what might have been their politic decision: to preserve him until he might be of high use again. Cassio is no Othello; the state has no replacement for the Moor, and might well have used him again, doubtless under some control. All of the rifts in Othello that Iago sensed and exploited are present in this final speech, but so is a final vision of judgment, one in which Othello abandons his nostalgias for glorious war, and pitifully seeks to expiate what cannot be expiated—not, at least, by a farewell to arms.

william shakespeare

othello

synopsis

Othello is a distinguished Moor, a black man, a brave and competent soldier, whose conduct of the Venetian wars against the Turks has raised him to the rank of general. He is now held in high esteem in Venice, and Brabantio, a rich and powerful senator, often invites him to his house, where he meets the fair, much-courted Desdemona, Brabantio's only child, who listens with rapt attention to the Moor's tales of adventures which the senator draws from him.

The strange nobility of this man of simple, commanding action fires the gentle girl's imagination, while her discerning mind so keenly appreciates his fine qualities that the natural barrier of race and color vanishes. With modest frankness, Desdemona shows Othello that she returns his love, and they are secretly married.

Cassio, a young soldier, who has often been the Moor's go-between in his courting, is promoted by Othello to be his chief lieutenant, a position coveted by his ensign, Iago, a crafty villainous man, who vows vengeance on both Othello and Cassio. Aided by Roderigo, a former lover of Desdemona's, he arouses Brabantio one night with a report of the elopement. Brabantio accuses the Moor of using witchcraft upon Desdemona, and orders him before the council which is meeting to discuss some disturbing reports of a large Turkish fleet now off the island of Cyprus, a Venetian stronghold. They had already summoned Othello, but now, when his services are imperatively needed, he stands before the Duke and council charged with a capital crime. The incensed Brabantio is heard respectfully, but his accusations are not always convincing, while Othello's story of his courting is told with such simple eloquence and directness that the Duke, as chief judge, refuses to condemn him, and he is given command of the expedition against the Turks.

Desdemona follows Othello to Cyprus in charge of Iago and his wife, Emilia, who, ignorant of her husband's hatred and schemes, becomes her mistress' devoted friend. A great storm wrecks the Turkish fleet, and Othello proclaims a holiday for rejoicing and for the celebration of his marriage, but he strictly charges Cassio to prevent excessive drinking or brawls among the soldiers which might disgust the people of Cyprus. Through Iago's wiles, the lieutenant himself becomes drunk. Roderigo precipitates a quarrel, rings an alarm bell and creates utmost confusion. Othello dismisses Cassio from his service, Iago urges the despairing young soldier to ask Desdemona to plead with her husband, and an interview is arranged between the lady and Cassio who hastens off when Othello approaches, lured to the spot by Iago who has promised to keep him away. Iago, in whose honesty and wisdom Othello has boundless faith, makes a rather ominous remark on the incident which returns to the Moor's brooding thoughts after he hears Desdemona's heartfelt appeal for Cassio. With consummate skill, Iago continues to drop hints and suggestions into Othello's ear. He speaks of Cassio's help with his courting, and of women's fickleness and ability to deceive, and stealthily torments his victim with insinuations of Cassio's passion for Desdemona.

One day Desdemona drops a beautiful handkerchief, her first gift from her husband who had begged her to guard it closely. It was a magical web, embroidered by a sibyl, which gave its possessor the power to hold her husband's love, and Othello's mother when dying had given it to him for his future wife. Emilia finds it, but Iago takes the handkerchief, and places it in Cassio's room; he then convinces Othello that Desdemona has given it to her lover. Desdemona, afraid to admit the loss of the precious heirloom, makes evasive replies when questioned by her distracted husband, now a ready target for Iago's last villainous shot. With Othello concealed close by, Iago beguiles the gay Cassio into a ribald conversation about his mistress, Bianca, while the Moor thinks his derision is levelled at Desdemona. By a stroke of evil luck, Bianca herself comes upon the scene, and Othello sees this woman of the streets scornfully hand back to Cassio his wife's handkerchief. Blind with rage, Othello orders Iago to kill Cassio. Iago kills Roderigo under cover of a street brawl, because he wants him out of the way, but he only maims Cassio.

Othello has but one thought, the destruction of Desdemona before she can betray other men. He goes to her bedchamber, and smothers his protesting wife to death. Emilia arrives in time to hear her lady breathe a few last words of devotion to her husband, who is now overwhelmed by the woman's testimony, Cassio's explanations, and the evidence of letters in the pockets of the dead Roderigo, proving Iago's villainy and his wife's innocence. Iago kills his wife for revealing his treachery, and is wounded by Othello. In his extreme anguish of soul, Othello falls upon his sword and dies at his wife's side. Cassio is made governor of Cyprus, with instructions from the council to torture and execute Iago under the utmost penalty of the law.

historical data

The original story of Othello is found in the novel *Il Moro de Venezia* from the *Hecatommithi* of Giraldo Cinthio, published in 1565. A French translation in 1584 was probably the edition with which Shakespeare was familiar. The novel may have been of Oriental origin, as it somewhat resembles the tale of *The Three Apples* in *The Thousand and One Nights.*

Shakespeare, in the main, followed the Italian romance, but reconstructed the catastrophe. He originated the names of all the personages, except that of Desdemona (the only name given by Cinthio), added the character of Roderigo; gave definite significance to Emilia; changed Iago from the conventional criminal of Italian fiction; and elevated Othello from Cinthio's conception of the savage Moor.

In the words of Sidney Lee, "The whole tragedy displays to magnificent advantage the dramatist's fully matured powers."

Othello was probably written in 1604, as an extract from *The Egerton Papers* notes that it was performed in August of that year at Harefield by Burbage's Players, before Queen Elizabeth, while she was on a visit to Sir Thomas Egerton, Lord Keeper of the Great Seal.

It was first published in quarto form, in 1622, and the following year appeared among "The Tragedies" in the First Folio.

dramatis personæ

Duke of Venice.

Brabantio, *a senator.*

Other Senators.

Gratiano, *brother to Brabantio.*

Lodovico, *kinsman to Brabantio.*

Othello, *a noble Moor in the service of the Venetian state.*

Cassio, *his lieutenant.*

Iago, *his ancient.*

Roderigo, *a Venetian gentleman.*

Montano, *Othello's predecessor in the government of Cyprus.*

Clown, *servant to Othello.*

Desdemona, *daughter to Brabantio and wife to Othello.*

Emilia, *wife to Iago.*

Bianca, *mistress to Cassio.*

Sailor, Messenger, Herald, Officers, Gentlemen, Musicians, and
Attendants.

Scene: Venice; a seaport in Cyprus.

act 1

scene 1. [*Venice. A street*]

Enter Roderigo *and* Iago

Roderigo. Tush, never tell me; I take it much unkindly
    That thou, Iago, who hast had my purse
    As if the strings were thine, shouldst know of this.

Iago. 'Sblood, but you will not hear me:
    If ever I did dream of such a matter,
    Abhor me.

Roderigo. Thou told'st me thou didst hold him in thy hate.

Iago. Despise me, if I do not. Three great ones of the city,
    In personal suit to make me his lieutenant,
    Off-capp'd to him, and, by the faith of man
    I know my price, I am worth no worse a place.
    But he, as loving his own pride and purposes,
    Evades them, with a bombast circumstance
    Horribly stuff'd with epithets of war,
    And, in conclusion
    Nonsuits my mediators. For 'Certes,' says he,
    'I have already chose my officer.'

And what was he?
Forsooth, a great arithmetician,
One Michael Cassio, a Florentine,
A fellow almost damn'd in a fair wife;
That never set a squadron in the field
Nor the division of a battle knows
More than a spinster—unless the bookish theoric,
Wherein the toged consuls can propose
As masterly as he. Mere prattle without practice
Is all his soldiership. But he, sir, had the election
And I, of whom his eyes had seen the proof
At Rhodes, at Cyprus, and on other grounds
Christian and heathen, must be be-lee'd and calm'd
By debitor and creditor. This counter-caster,
He, in good time must his lieutenant be
And I—God bless the mark!—his Moorship's ancient.

Roderigo. By heaven, I rather would have been his hangman.

Iago. Why, there's no remedy; 'tis the curse of service,
Preferment goes by letter and affection,
And not by old gradation, where each second
Stood heir to the first. Now, sir, be judge yourself
Whether I in any just term am affined
To love the Moor.

Roderigo.   I would not follow him then.

Iago. O, sir, content you;
I follow him to serve my turn upon him.
We cannot all be masters, nor all masters
Cannot be truly follow'd. You shall mark
Many a duteous and knee-crooking knave
That doting on his own obsequious bondage
Wears out his time, much like his master's ass,
For nought but provender, and when he's old, cashier'd.

Whip me such honest knaves. Others there are
Who, trimm'd in forms and visages of duty,
Keep yet their hearts attending on themselves,
And throwing but shows of service on their lords
Do well thrive by them, and when they have lined their coats
Do themselves homage: these fellows have some soul,
And such a one do I profess myself.
For, sir,
It is as sure as you are Roderigo,
Were I the Moor, I would not be Iago:
In following him, I follow but myself;
Heaven is my judge, not I for love and duty
But seeming so, for my peculiar end.
For when my outward action doth demonstrate
The native act and figure of my heart
In compliment extern, 'tis not long after
But I will wear my heart upon my sleeve
For daws to peck at: I am not what I am.

Roderigo. What a full fortune does the thick-lips owe,
If he can carry't thus!

Iago.   Call up her father,
Rouse him: make after him, poison his delight,
Proclaim him in the streets, incense her kinsmen,
And, though he in a fertile climate dwell,
Plague him with flies. Though that his joy be joy,
Yet throw such changes of vexation on't
As it may lose some colour.

Roderigo. Here is her father's house; I'll call aloud.

Iago. Do, with like timorous accent and dire yell
As when, by night and negligence, the fire
Is spied in populous cities.

Roderigo. What, ho, Brabantio! Signior Brabantio, ho!

Iago. Awake! What, ho, Brabantio! Thieves, thieves, thieves!
   Look to your house, your daughter and your bags!
   Thieves! Thieves!

>   Brabantio *appears above, at a window*

Brabantio. What is the reason of this terrible summons?
   What is the matter there?

Roderigo. Signior, is all your family within?

Iago. Are your doors lock'd?

Brabantio.   Why, wherefore ask you this?

Iago. 'Zounds, sir, you're robb'd; for shame, put on your gown;
   Your heart is burst, you have lost half your soul.
   Even now, now, very now, an old black ram
   Is tupping your white ewe. Arise, arise,
   Awake the snorting citizens with the bell,
   Or else the devil will make a grandsire of you.
   Arise, I say!

Brabantio.   What, have you lost your wits?

Roderigo. Most reverend signior, do you know my voice?

Brabantio. Not I, what are you?

Roderigo. My name is Roderigo.

Brabantio.   The worser welcome.
   I have charged thee not to haunt about my doors:
   In honest plainness thou hast heard me say
   My daughter is not for thee; and now in madness,
   Being full of supper and distempering draughts,
   Upon malicious bravery dost thou come
   To start my quiet.

Roderigo. Sir, sir, sir—

Brabantio. But thou must needs be sure
   My spirit and my place have in them power
   To make this bitter to thee.

Roderigo. Patience, good sir.

Brabantio. What tell'st thou me of robbing? This is Venice;
   My house is not a grange.

Roderigo. Most grave Brabantio,
   In simple and pure soul I come to you.

Iago. 'Zounds, sir, you are one of those that will not serve God, if
   the devil bid you. Because we come to do you service and you
   think we are ruffians, you'll have your daughter covered with a
   Barbary horse; you'll have your nephews neigh to you; you'll
   have coursers for cousins, and gennets for germans.

Brabantio. What profane wretch art thou?

Iago. I am one, sir, that comes to tell you your daughter and the
   Moor are now making the beast with two backs.

Brabantio. Thou art a villain.

Iago. You are—a senator.

Brabantio. This thou shalt answer; I know thee, Roderigo.

Roderigo. Sir, I will answer any thing. But, I beseech you,
   If 't be your pleasure and most wise consent,
   As partly I find it is, that your fair daughter
   At this odd-even and dull watch o' the night,
   Transported with no worse nor better guard
   But with a knave of common hire, a gondolier,
   To the gross clasps of a lascivious Moor—
   If this be known to you, and your allowance,
   We then have done you bold and saucy wrongs.
   But if you know not this, my manners tell me
   We have your wrong rebuke. Do not believe
   That from the sense of all civility

I thus would play and trifle with your reverence.
Your daughter, if you have not given her leave,
I say again, hath made a gross revolt,
Tying her duty, beauty, wit and fortunes
In an extravagant and wheeling stranger
Of here and every where. Straight satisfy yourself:
If she be in her chamber or your house,
Let loose on me the justice of the state
For thus deluding you.

Brabantio.   Strike on the tinder, ho!
Give me a taper! Call up all my people!
This accident is not unlike my dream:
Belief of it oppresses me already.
Light, I say! Light!

Exit above.

Iago.   Farewell, for I must leave you.
It seems not meet, nor wholesome to my place,
To be produced—as, if I stay, I shall—
Against the Moor. For I do know the state,
However this may gall him with some check,
Cannot with safety cast him, for he's embark'd
With such loud reason to the Cyprus wars,
Which even now stands in act, that for their souls
Another of his fathom they have none
To lead their business—in which regard,
Though I do hate him as I do hell pains,
Yet for necessity of present life
I must show out a flag and sign of love,
Which is indeed but sign. That you shall surely find him,
Lead to the Sagittary the raised search,
And there will I be with him. So farewell.

Exit.

Enter, below, Brabantio, *in his night-gown, and*
Servants *with torches*

Brabantio. It is too true an evil: gone she is,
    And what's to come of my despised time
    Is nought but bitterness. Now, Roderigo,
    Where didst thou see her? O unhappy girl!
    With the Moor, say'st thou? Who would be a father!
    How didst thou know 'twas she? O, she deceives me
    Past thought! What said she to you? Get more tapers.
    Raise all my kindred. Are they married, think you?

Roderigo. Truly, I think they are.

Brabantio. O heaven! How got she out? O treason of the blood!
    Fathers, from hence trust not your daughters' minds
    By what you see them act. Is there not charms
    By which the property of youth and maidhood
    May be abused? Have you not read, Roderigo,
    Of some such thing?

Roderigo.   Yes, sir, I have indeed.

Brabantio. Call up my brother. O, would you had had her!
    Some one way, some another. Do you know
    Where we may apprehend her and the Moor?

Roderigo. I think I can discover him, if you please
    To get good guard and go along with me.

Brabantio. Pray you, lead on. At every house I'll call;
    I may command at most. Get weapons, ho!
    And raise some special officers of night.
    On, good Roderigo; I'll deserve your pains.

Exeunt.

scene 2.   [*Another street*]

Enter Othello, Iago, *and* Attendants *with torches*

Iago. Though in the trade of war I have slain men,
    Yet do I hold it very stuff o' th' conscience
    To do no contrived murder: I lack iniquity
    Sometimes to do me service. Nine or ten times
    I had thought to have yerk'd him here under the ribs.

Othello. 'Tis better as it is.

Iago.   Nay, but he prated
    And spoke such scurvy and provoking terms
    Against your honour,
    That with the little godliness I have
    I did full hard forbear him. But I pray you, sir,
    Are you fast married? Be assured of this,
    That the magnifico is much beloved,
    And hath in his effect a voice potential
    As double as the duke's. He will divorce you
    Or put upon you what restraint and grievance
    The law, with all his might to enforce it on,
    Will give him cable.

Othello.   Let him do his spite;
    My services, which I have done the signiory,
    Shall out-tongue his complaints. 'Tis yet to know—
    Which, when I know that boasting is an honour,
    I shall promulgate—I fetch my life and being
    From men of royal siege, and my demerits
    May speak unbonneted to as proud a fortune
    As this that I have reach'd. For know, Iago,
    But that I love the gentle Desdemona,

I would not my unhoused free condition
Put into circumscription and confine
For the sea's worth. But look, what lights come yond?

Iago. Those are the raised father and his friends;
You were best go in.

Othello.   Not I, I must be found.
My parts, my title and my perfect soul
Shall manifest me rightly. Is it they?

Iago. By Janus, I think no.
                Enter Cassio, *and certain* Officers *with torches*

Othello. The servants of the duke, and my lieutenant.
The goodness of the night upon you, friends!
What is the news?

Cassio.   The duke does greet you, general,
And he requires your haste-post-haste appearance,
Even on the instant.

Othello.   What is the matter, think you?

Cassio. Something from Cyprus, as I may divine:
It is a business of some heat. The galleys
Have sent a dozen sequent messengers
This very night at one another's heels,
And many of the consuls, raised and met,
Are at the duke's already: you have been hotly call'd for;
When, being not at your lodging to be found,
The senate hath sent about three several quests
To search you out.

Othello.   'Tis well I am found by you.
I will but spend a word here in the house,
And go with you.

                                        Exit.

Cassio. Ancient, what makes he here?

Iago. Faith, he to-night hath boarded a land carack:
  If it prove lawful prize, he's made for ever.

Cassio. I do not understand.

Iago. He's married.

Cassio. To who?

Re-enter Othello

Iago. Marry, to—Come, captain, will you go?

Othello. Have with you.

Cassio. Here comes another troop to seek for you.

Iago. It is Brabantio: general, be advised,
  He comes to bad intent.

Enter Brabantio, Roderigo, *and* Officers
with torches and weapons

Othello. Holla! Stand there!

Roderigo. Signior, it is the Moor.

Brabantio. Down with him, thief!

They draw on both sides.

Iago. You, Roderigo! Come, sir, I am for you.

Othello. Keep up your bright swords, for the dew will rust them.
  Good signior, you shall more command with years
  Than with your weapons.

Brabantio. O thou foul thief, where hast thou stow'd my daughter?
  Damn'd as thou art, thou hast enchanted her,
  For I'll refer me to all things of sense
  If she in chains of magic were not bound,
  Whether a maid so tender, fair and happy,
  So opposite to marriage that she shunn'd
  The wealthy curled darlings of our nation,

Would ever have, t' incur a general mock,
Run from her guardage to the sooty bosom
Of such a thing as thou, to fear, not to delight.
Judge me the world, if 'tis not gross in sense
That thou hast practised on her with foul charms,
Abused her delicate youth with drugs or minerals
That weaken motion: I'll have 't disputed on;
'Tis probable, and palpable to thinking.
I therefore apprehend and do attach thee
For an abuser of the world, a practiser
Of arts inhibited and out of warrant.
Lay hold upon him: if he do resist,
Subdue him at his peril.

Othello.   Hold your hands,
Both you of my inclining and the rest:
Were it my cue to fight, I should have known it
Without a prompter. Where will you that I go
To answer this your charge?

Brabantio.   To prison, till fit time
Of law and course of direct session
Call thee to answer.

Othello.   What if I do obey?
How may the duke be therewith satisfied,
Whose messengers are here about my side
Upon some present business of the state
To bring me to him?

First Officer.   'Tis true, most worthy signior;
The duke's in council, and your noble self,
I am sure, is sent for.

Brabantio.   How! The duke in council?
In this time of the night! Bring him away:
Mine's not an idle cause. The duke himself,

Or any of my brothers of the state,
Cannot but feel this wrong as 'twere their own,
For if such actions may have passage free,
Bond-slaves and pagans shall our statesmen be.

Exeunt.

scene 3. [*A council-chamber*]

The Duke *and* Senators *sitting at a table;* Officers *attending*

Duke. There is no composition in these news
  That gives them credit.

First Senator.   Indeed they are disproportion'd;
  My letters say a hundred and seven galleys.

Duke. And mine, a hundred and forty.

Second Senator.   And mine, two hundred:
  But though they jump not on a just account—
  As in these cases, where the aim reports,
  'Tis oft with difference—yet do they all confirm
  A Turkish fleet, and bearing up to Cyprus.

Duke. Nay, it is possible enough to judgement:
  I do not so secure me in the error,
  But the main article I do approve
  In fearful sense.

Sailor. [*Within*] What, ho! What ho! What ho!

First Officer. A messenger from the galleys.

                Enter Sailor

Duke.   Now, what's the business?

Sailor. The Turkish preparation makes for Rhodes,
  So was I bid report here to the state
  By Signior Angelo.

Duke. How say you by this change?

First Senator.   This cannot be,
   By no assay of reason: 'tis a pageant
   To keep us in false gaze. When we consider
   Th' importancy of Cyprus to the Turk,
   And let ourselves again but understand
   That as it more concerns the Turk than Rhodes,
   So may he with more facile question bear it,
   For that it stands not in such warlike brace
   But altogether lacks th' abilities
   That Rhodes is dress'd in. If we make thought of this,
   We must not think the Turk is so unskillful
   To leave that latest which concerns him first,
   Neglecting an attempt of ease and gain
   To wake and wage a danger profitless.

Duke. Nay, in all confidence, he's not for Rhodes.

First Officer. Here is more news.

Enter a Messenger

Messenger. The Ottomites, reverend and gracious,
   Steering with due course toward the isle of Rhodes,
   Have there injointed them with an after fleet.

First Senator. Ay, so I thought. How many, as you guess?

Messenger. Of thirty sail: and now they do re-stem
   Their backward course, bearing with frank appearance
   Their purposes toward Cyprus. Signior Montano,
   Your trusty and most valiant servitor,
   With his free duty recommends you thus,
   And prays you to 'elieve him.

Duke. 'Tis certain then for Cyprus.
   Marcus Luccicos, is not he in town?

First Senator. He's now in Florence.

Duke. Write from us to him; post–post–haste dispatch.

First Senator. Here comes Brabantio and the valiant Moor.
    Enter Brabantio, Othello, Iago, Roderigo, *and* Officers

Duke. Valiant Othello, we must straight employ you
    Against the general enemy Ottoman.
    [*To Brabantio*] I did not see you; welcome, gentle signior,
    We lack'd your counsel and your help tonight.

Brabantio. So did I yours. Good your grace, pardon me;
    Neither my place nor aught I heard of business
    Hath raised me from my bed, nor doth the general care
    Take hold on me; for my particular grief
    Is of so flood–gate and o'erbearing nature
    That it engluts and swallows other sorrows
    And it is still itself.

Duke.   Why, what's the matter?

Brabantio. My daughter! O, my daughter!

All.   Dead?

Brabantio.   Ay, to me;
    She is abused, stol'n from me and corrupted
    By spells and medicines bought of mountebanks,
    For nature so preposterously to err,
    Being not deficient, blind, or lame of sense,
    Sans witchcraft could not.

Duke. Whoe'er he be that in this foul proceeding
    Hath thus beguiled your daughter of herself
    And you of her, the bloody book of law
    You shall yourself read in the bitter letter
    After your own sense, yea, though our proper son
    Stood in your action.

Brabantio.   Humbly I thank your grace.
    Here is the man, this Moor, whom now it seems

Your special mandate for the state affairs.
Hath hither brought.

All.   We are very sorry for 't.

Duke. [*To Othello*] What in your own part can you say to this?

Brabantio. Nothing, but this is so.

Othello. Most potent, grave, and reverend signiors,
    My very noble and approved good masters,
    That I have ta'en away this old man's daughter,
    It is most true; true, I have married her.
    The very head and front of my offending
    Hath this extent, no more. Rude am I in my speech
    And little blest with the soft phrase of peace,
    For since these arms of mine had seven years pith
    Till now some nine moons wasted, they have used
    Their dearest action in the tented field,
    And little of this great world can I speak
    More than pertains to feats of broil and battle,
    And therefore little shall I grace my cause
    In speaking for myself. Yet, by your gracious patience,
    I will a round unvarnish'd tale deliver
    Of my whole course of love, what drugs, what charms,
    What conjuration and what mighty magic—
    For such proceeding I am charged withal—
    I won his daughter.

Brabantio.   A maiden never bold,
    Of spirit so still and quiet that her motion
    Blush'd at herself; and she—in spite of nature,
    Of years, of country, credit, everything—
    To fall in love with what she fear'd to look on!
    It is a judgement maim'd and most imperfect,
    That will confess perfection so could err
    Against all rules of nature, and must be driven

To find out practices of cunning hell,
Why this should be. I therefore vouch again
That with some mixtures powerful o'er the blood,
Or with some dram conjured to this effect,
He wrought upon her.

Duke.   To vouch this is no proof,
Without more certain and more overt test
Than these thin habits and poor likelihoods
Of modern seeming do prefer against him.

First Senator. But, Othello, speak:
Did you by indirect and forced courses
Subdue and poison this young maid's affections?
Or came it by request, and such fair question
As soul to soul affordeth?

Othello.   I do beseech you,
Send for the lady to the Sagittary,
And let her speak of me before her father.
If you do find me foul in her report,
The trust, the office I do hold of you
Not only take away, but let your sentence
Even fall upon my life.

Duke.   Fetch Desdemona hither.

Othello. Ancient, conduct them; you best know the place.

                              Exeunt Iago *and* Attendants.
And till she come, as truly as to heaven
I do confess the vices of my blood,
So justly to your grave ears I'll present
How I did thrive in this fair lady's love
And she in mine.

Duke. Say it, Othello.

Othello. Her father loved me, oft invited me,
Still question'd me the story of my life

From year to year, the battles, sieges, fortunes
That I have pass'd.
I ran it through, even from my boyish days
To the very moment that he bade me tell it,
Wherein I spake of most disastrous chances,
Of moving accidents by flood and field,
Of hair-breadth 'scapes i' th' imminent deadly breach,
Of being taken by the insolent foe
And sold to slavery, of my redemption thence,
And portance in my travels' history:
Wherein of antres vast and deserts idle,
Rough quarries, rocks, and hills whose heads touch heaven,
It was my hint to speak—such was the process—
And of the Cannibals that each other eat,
The Anthropophagi, and men whose heads
Do grow beneath their shoulders. This to hear
Would Desdemona seriously incline,
But still the house-affairs would draw her thence;
Which ever as she could with haste dispatch
She'd come again, and with a greedy ear
Devour up my discourse, which I observing,
Took once a pliant hour and found good means
To draw from her a prayer of earnest heart
That I would all my pilgrimage dilate,
Whereof by parcels she had something heard,
But not intentively. I did consent,
And often did beguile her of her tears
When I did speak of some distressful stroke
That my youth suffer'd. My story being done,
She gave me for my pains a world of sighs:
She swore in faith 'twas strange, 'twas passing strange;
'Twas pitiful, 'twas wondrous pitiful.
She wish'd she had not heard it, yet she wish'd

That heaven had made her such a man. She thank'd me
And bade me, if I had a friend that loved her,
I should but teach him how to tell my story,
And that would woo her. Upon this hint I spake:
She loved me for the dangers I had pass'd,
And I loved her that she did pity them.
This only is the witchcraft I have used.
Here comes the lady; let her witness it.

Enter Desdemona, Iago, *and* Attendants

Duke. I think this tale would win my daughter too.
Good Brabantio,
Take up this mangled matter at the best:
Men do their broken weapons rather use
Than their bare hands.

Brabantio.   I pray you, hear her speak:
If she confess that she was half the wooer,
Destruction on my head, if my bad blame
Light on the man! Come hither, gentle mistress:
Do you perceive in all this noble company
Where most you owe obedience?

Desdemona.   My noble father,
I do perceive here a divided duty.
To you I am bound for life and education:
My life and education both do learn me
How to respect you; you are the lord of duty,
I am hitherto your daughter. But here's my husband,
And so much duty as my mother show'd
To you, preferring you before her father,
So much I challenge that I may profess
Due to the Moor my lord.

Brabantio.   God be with you. I have done.
Please it your grace, on to the state affairs:

I had rather to adopt a child than get it.
Come hither, Moor:
I here do give thee that with all my heart
Which, but thou hast already, with all my heart
I would keep from thee. For your sake, jewel,
I am glad at soul I have no other child,
For thy escape would teach me tyranny,
To hang clogs on them. I have done, my lord.

Duke. Let me speak like yourself, and lay a sentence
Which, as a grise or step, may help these lovers
Into your favour.
When remedies are past, the griefs are ended
By seeing the worst which late on hopes depended.
To mourn a mischief that is past and gone
Is the next way to draw new mischief on.
What cannot be preserved when fortune takes,
Patience her injury a mockery makes.
The robb'd that smiles steals something from the thief;
He robs himself that spends a bootless grief.

Brabantio. So let the Turk of Cyprus us beguile;
We lose it not so long as we can smile.
He bears the sentence well, that nothing bears
But the free comfort which from thence he hears.
But he bears both the sentence and the sorrow
That, to pay grief, must of poor patience borrow.
These sentences, to sugar or to gall,
Being strong on both sides, are equivocal.
But words are words: I never yet did hear
That the bruised heart was pierced through the ear.
I humbly beseech you, proceed to th' affairs of state.

Duke. The Turk with a most mighty preparation makes for
Cyprus. Othello, the fortitude of the place is best known to

you, and though we have there a substitute of most allowed
sufficiency, yet opinion, a sovereign mistress of effects, throws
a more safer voice on you. You must therefore be content to
slubber the gloss of your new fortunes with this more
stubborn and boisterous expedition.

Othello. The tyrant custom, most grave senators,
Hath made the flinty and steel couch of war
My thrice-driven bed of down. I do agnize
A natural and prompt alacrity
I find in hardness, and do undertake
These present wars against the Ottomites.
Most humbly therefore, bending to your state,
I crave fit disposition for my wife,
Due reference of place and exhibition,
With such accommodation and besort
As levels with her breeding.

Duke.   If you please,
Be't at her father's.

Brabantio.   I'll not have it so.

Othello. Nor I.

Desdemona.   Nor would I there reside,
To put my father in impatient thoughts
By being in his eye. Most gracious duke,
To my unfolding lend your prosperous ear
And let me find a charter in your voice
To assist my simpleness.

Duke. What would you, Desdemona?

Desdemona. That I did love the Moor to live with him,
My downright violence and storm of fortunes
May trumpet to the world. My heart's subdued
Even to the very quality of my lord:

I saw Othello's visage in his mind,
And to his honours and his valiant parts
Did I my soul and fortunes consecrate.
So that, dear lords, if I be left behind,
A moth of peace, and he go to the war,
The rites for which I love him are bereft me,
And I a heavy interim shall support
By his dear absence. Let me go with him.

Othello. Let her have your voice.
Vouch with me, heaven, I therefore beg it not
To please the palate of my appetite,
Nor to comply with heat—the young affects
In me defunct—and proper satisfaction,
But to be free and bounteous to her mind.
And heaven defend your good souls, that you think
I will your serious and great business scant
For she is with me. No, when light-wing'd toys
Of feather'd Cupid seel with wanton dullness
My speculative and officed instrument,
That my disports corrupt and taint my business,
Let housewives make a skillet of my helm,
And all indign and base adversities
Make head against my estimation!

Duke. Be it as you shall privately determine,
Either for her stay or going: th' affair cries haste,
And speed must answer 't; you must hence to-night.

Desdemona. Tonight, my lord?

Duke.   This night.

Othello.   With all my heart.

Duke. At nine i' the morning here we'll meet again.
Othello, leave some officer behind
And he shall our commission bring to you,

With such things else of quality and respect
As doth import you.

Othello.   So please your grace, my ancient;
A man he is of honesty and trust.
To his conveyance I assign my wife,
With what else needful your good grace shall think
To be sent after me.

Duke.   Let it be so.
Good night to every one.
[*To Brabantio*] And, noble signior,
If virtue no delighted beauty lack,
Your son-in-law is far more fair than black.

First Senator. Adieu, brave Moor; use Desdemona well.

Brabantio. Look to her, Moor, if thou hast eyes to see:
She has deceived her father, and may thee.

                              Exeunt Duke, Senators, Officers, *&c.*

Othello. My life upon her faith! Honest Iago,
My Desdemona must I leave to thee:
I prithee, let thy wife attend on her,
And bring them after in the best advantage.
Come, Desdemona, I have but an hour
Of love, of worldly matters and direction
To spend with thee: we must obey the time.

                              Exeunt Othello *and* Desdemona.

Roderigo. Iago!

Iago. What say'st thou, noble heart?

Roderigo. What will I do, thinkest thou?

Iago. Why, go to bed and sleep.

Roderigo. I will incontinently drown myself.

Iago. If thou dost, I shall never love thee after.
Why, thou silly gentleman!

Roderigo. It is silliness to live when to live is torment; and then have we a prescription to die when death is our physician.

Iago. O villanous! I have looked upon the world for four times seven years, and since I could distinguish betwixt a benefit and an injury, I never found man that knew how to love himself. Ere I would say I would drown myself for the love of a guinea-hen, I would change my humanity with a baboon.

Roderigo. What should I do? I confess it is my shame to be so fond, but it is not in my virtue to amend it.

Iago. Virtue? A fig! 'tis in ourselves that we are thus or thus. Our bodies are gardens, to the which our wills are gardeners. So that if we will plant nettles or sow lettuce, set hyssop and weed up thyme, supply it with one gender of herbs or distract it with many, either to have it sterile with idleness or manured with industry—why, the power and corrigible authority of this lies in our wills. If the balance of our lives had not one scale of reason to poise another of sensuality, the blood and baseness of our natures would conduct us to most preposterous conclusions. But we have reason to cool our raging motions, our carnal stings, our unbitted lusts; whereof I take this, that you call love, to be a sect or scion.

Roderigo. It cannot be.

Iago. It is merely a lust of the blood and a permission of the will. Come, be a man: drown thyself? Drown cats and blind puppies. I have professed me thy friend, and I confess me knit to thy deserving with cables of perdurable toughness. I could never better stead thee than now. Put money in thy purse, follow thou the wars, defeat thy favour with an usurped beard; I say, put money in thy purse. It cannot be that Desdemona should long continue her love to the Moor—put money in thy purse—nor he his to her: it was a violent commencement, and thou shalt see an answerable sequestration; put but money in thy purse. These Moors are changeable in their wills:—fill thy purse with money. The food that to him now is as luscious as locusts, shall be to him shortly as acerb as coloquintida. She must change for youth; when she is sated with his body, she will find the error of her choice: she must have change, she must. Therefore put money in thy purse. If thou wilt needs damn thyself, do it a more delicate way than drowning. Make all the money thou canst: if sanctimony and a frail vow betwixt an erring barbarian and a supersubtle Venetian be not too hard for my wits and all the tribe of hell, thou shalt enjoy her; therefore make money. A pox of drowning thyself! It is clean out of the way: seek thou rather to be hanged in compassing thy joy than to be drowned and go without her.

Roderigo. Wilt thou be fast to my hopes, if I depend on the issue?

Iago. Thou art sure of me: go, make money. I have told thee often, and I re-tell thee again and again, I hate the Moor. My cause is hearted; thine hath no less reason. Let us be conjunctive in our revenge against him. If thou canst cuckold him, thou dost thyself a pleasure, me a sport. There are many events in the womb of time, which will be delivered. Traverse, go, provide thy money. We will have more of this tomorrow. Adieu.

Roderigo. Where shall we meet i' the morning?

Iago. At my lodging.

Roderigo. I'll be with thee betimes.

Iago. Go to; farewell. Do you hear, Roderigo?

Roderigo. What say you?

Iago. No more of drowning, do you hear?

Roderigo. I am changed: I'll go sell all my land.

Exit.

Iago. Thus do I ever make my fool my purse,
    For I mine own gain'd knowledge should profane
    If I would time expend with such a snipe
    But for my sport and profit. I hate the Moor,
    And it is thought abroad that 'twixt my sheets
    He has done my office. I know not if 't be true,
    But I for mere suspicion in that kind
    Will do as if for surety. He holds me well;
    The better shall my purpose work on him.
    Cassio's a proper man: let me see now,
    To get his place, and to plume up my will
    In double knavery—How, how?—Let's see:—
    After some time, to abuse Othello's ear
    That he is too familiar with his wife.
    He hath a person and a smooth dispose
    To be suspected, framed to make women false.
    The Moor is of a free and open nature,
    That thinks men honest that but seem to be so,
    And will as tenderly be led by the nose
    As asses are.
    I have't. It is engender'd. Hell and night
    Must bring this monstrous birth to the world's light.

                        Exit.

act 2

[*A sea-port in Cyprus. An open place near the quay*]

Enter Montano *and two* Gentlemen

Montano. What from the cape can you discern at sea?

First Gentleman. Nothing at all, it is a high-wrought flood;
   I cannot 'twixt the heaven and the main
   Descry a sail.

Montano. Methinks the wind hath spoke aloud at land;
   A fuller blast ne'er shook our battlements:
   If it hath ruffian'd so upon the sea,
   What ribs of oak, when mountains melt on them,
   Can hold the mortise? What shall we hear of this?

Second Gentleman. A segregation of the Turkish fleet:
   For do but stand upon the foaming shore,
   The chidden billow seems to pelt the clouds,
   The wind-shaked surge, with high and monstrous mane,
   Seems to cast water on the burning bear
   And quench the guards of the ever-fixed pole.
   I never did like molestation view
   On the enchafed flood.

Montano.　　　　　　　　If that the Turkish fleet
　　Be not enshelter'd and embay'd, they are drown'd.
　　It is impossible to bear it out.

　　　　　　　　Enter a third Gentleman

Third Gentleman. News, lads! Our wars are done!
　　The desperate tempest hath so bang'd the Turks,
　　That their designment halts. A noble ship of Venice
　　Hath seen a grievous wrack and sufferance
　　On most part of their fleet.

Montano. How! Is this true?

Third Gentleman.　　　　　　The ship is here put in,
　　A Veronesa; Michael Cassio,
　　Lieutenant to the warlike Moor Othello,
　　Is come on shore; the Moor himself at sea,
　　And is in full commission here for Cyprus.

Montano. I am glad on't, 'tis a worthy governor.

Third Gentleman. But this same Cassio, though he speak of
　　comfort
　　Touching the Turkish loss, yet he looks sadly
　　And prays the Moor be safe, for they were parted
　　With foul and violent tempest.

Montano.　　　　　　　　Pray heavens he be,
　　For I have served him, and the man commands
　　Like a full soldier. Let's to the seaside, ho!
　　As well to see the vessel that's come in
　　As to throw out our eyes for brave Othello,
　　Even till we make the main and th' aerial blue
　　An indistinct regard.

Third Gentleman.　　　Come, let's do so,
　　For every minute is expectancy
　　Of more arrivance.

Enter Cassio

Cassio. Thanks, you the valiant of this warlike isle
   That so approve the Moor! O, let the heavens
   Give him defence against the elements,
   For I have lost him on a dangerous sea.

Montano. Is he well shipp'd?

Cassio. His bark is stoutly timber'd, and his pilot
   Of very expert and approved allowance,
   Therefore my hopes, not surfeited to death,
   Stand in bold cure.

                              A cry within: "A sail, a sail, a sail!"

                    Enter a fourth Gentleman

Cassio. What noise?

Fourth Gentleman. The town is empty; on the brow o' th' sea
   Stand ranks of people, and they cry 'A sail!'

Cassio. My hopes do shape him for the governor.

                                        Guns heard.

Second Gentleman. They do discharge their shot of courtesy:
   Our friends at least.

Cassio.   I pray you sir, go forth,
   And give us truth who 'tis that is arrived.

Second Gentleman. I shall.

                                              Exit.

Montano. But, good lieutenant, is your general wived?

Cassio. Most fortunately: he hath achieved a maid
   That paragons description and wild fame;
   One that excels the quirks of blazoning pens,
   And in the essential vesture of creation
   Does tire the ingener.

                    Re-enter second Gentleman
                    How now! Who has put in?

Second Gentleman. 'Tis one Iago, ancient to the general.

Cassio. He's had most favourable and happy speed,
Tempests themselves, high seas, and howling winds,
The gutter'd rocks, and congregated sands,
Traitors ensteep'd to clog the guiltless keel,
As having sense of beauty, do omit
Their mortal natures, letting go safely by
The divine Desdemona.

Montano.   What is she?

Cassio. She that I spake of, our great captain's captain,
Left in the conduct of the bold Iago;
Whose footing here anticipates our thoughts
A se'nnight's speed. Great Jove, Othello guard,
And swell his sail with thine own powerful breath
That he may bless this bay with his tall ship,
Make love's quick pants in Desdemona's arms,
Give renew'd fire to our extincted spirits,
And bring all Cyprus comfort.
    Enter Desdemona, Emilia, Iago, Roderigo, *and* Attendants
                              O, behold,
The riches of the ship is come on shore!
Ye men of Cyprus, let her have your knees.
Hail to thee, lady! And the grace of heaven,
Before, behind thee, and on every hand,
Enwheel thee round!

Desdemona.   I thank you, valiant Cassio.
What tidings can you tell me of my lord?

Cassio. He is not yet arrived, nor know I aught
But that he's well and will be shortly here.

Desdemona. O, but I fear—How lost you company?

Cassio. The great contention of the sea and skies
    Parted our fellowship—But, hark! A sail!

                          A cry within: "A sail, a sail!" Guns heard.

Second Gentleman. They give their greeting to the citadel:
    This likewise is a friend.

Cassio.   See for the news.

                                Exit Gentleman.

    Good ancient, you are welcome.
    [*To Emilia*] Welcome, mistress.
    Let it not gall your patience, good Iago,
    That I extend my manners; 'tis my breeding
    That gives me this bold show of courtesy.

                            Kisses Emilia.

Iago. Sir, would she give you so much of her lips
    As of her tongue she oft bestows on me,
    You'd have enough.

Desdemona.   Alas, she has no speech.

Iago. In faith, too much;
    I find it still when I have list to sleep.
    Marry, before your ladyship, I grant,
    She puts her tongue a little in her heart
    And chides with thinking.

Emilia. You have little cause to say so.

Iago. Come on, come on, you are pictures out of doors,
    Bells in your parlours, wild-cats in your kitchens,
    Saints in your injuries, devils being offended,
    Players in your housewifery, and housewives in your beds.

Desdemona. O, fie upon thee, slanderer!

Iago. Nay, it is true, or else I am a Turk:
    You rise to play, and go to bed to work.

Emilia. You shall not write my praise.

Iago.   No, let me not.

Desdemona. What wouldst thou write of me, if thou shouldst
praise me?

Iago. O gentle lady, do not put me to't;
For I am nothing if not critical.

Desdemona. Come on, assay—There's one gone to the harbour?

Iago. Ay, madam.

Desdemona. I am not merry, but I do beguile
The thing I am by seeming otherwise.
Come, how wouldst thou praise me?

Iago. I am about it, but indeed my invention
Comes from my pate as birdlime does from frieze;
It plucks out brains and all. But my Muse labours,
And thus she is deliver'd.
If she be fair and wise, fairness and wit,
The one's for use, the other useth it.

Desdemona. Well praised! How if she be black and witty?

Iago. If she be black, and thereto have a wit,
She'll find a white that shall her blackness fit.

Desdemona. Worse and worse.

Emilia. How if fair and foolish?

Iago. She never yet was foolish that was fair;
For even her folly help'd her to an heir.

Desdemona. These are old fond paradoxes to make fools laugh
i' th' alehouse. What miserable praise hast thou for her that's
foul and foolish?

Iago. There's none so foul, and foolish thereunto,
But does foul pranks which fair and wise ones do.

Desdemona. O heavy ignorance! Thou praisest the worst best. But what praise couldst thou bestow on a deserving woman indeed, one that in the authority of her merit did justly put on the vouch of very malice itself?

Iago. She that was ever fair and never proud,
   Had tongue at will and yet was never loud,
   Never lack'd gold and yet went never gay,
   Fled from her wish and yet said 'Now I may';
   She that, being anger'd, her revenge being nigh,
   Bade her wrong stay and her displeasure fly;
   She that in wisdom never was so frail
   To change the cod's head for the salmon's tail;
   She that could think and ne'er disclose her mind,
   See suitors following and not look behind;
   She was a wight, if ever such wight were—

Desdemona. To do what?

Iago. To suckle fools and chronicle small beer.

Desdemona. O most lame and impotent conclusion! Do not learn of him, Emilia, though he be thy husband. How say you, Cassio? Is he not a most profane and liberal counsellor?

Cassio. He speaks home, madam: you may relish him more in the soldier than in the scholar.

Iago. [*Aside*] He takes her by the palm: ay, well said, whisper. With as little a web as this will I ensnare as great a fly as Cassio. Ay, smile upon her, do: I will gyve thee in thine own courtship. You say true, 'tis so, indeed. If such tricks as these strip you out of your lieutenantry, it had been better you had not kissed your three fingers so oft, which now again you are most apt to play the sir in. Very good, well kissed! An excellent courtesy! 'tis so, indeed. Yet again your fingers to your lips? Would they were clyster-pipes for your sake!— [*Trumpet within.*] The Moor! I know his trumpet.

Cassio. 'Tis truly so.

Desdemona. Let's meet him and receive him.

Cassio. Lo, where he comes!

      Enter Othello *and* Attendants

Othello. O my fair warrior!

Desdemona.   My dear Othello!

Othello. It gives me wonder great as my content
 To see you here before me. O my soul's joy!
 If after every tempest come such calms,
 May the winds blow till they have waken'd death!
 And let the labouring bark climb hills of seas
 Olympus-high, and duck again as low
 As hell's from heaven! If it were now to die,
 'Twere now to be most happy, for I fear,
 My soul hath her content so absolute
 That not another comfort like to this
 Succeeds in unknown fate.

Desdemona.   The heavens forbid
 But that our loves and comforts should increase,
 Even as our days do grow!

Othello.   Amen to that, sweet powers!
 I cannot speak enough of this content;
 It stops me here; it is too much of joy.
 And this, and this, the greatest discords be

             Kissing her.

 That e'er our hearts shall make!

Iago. [*Aside*]   O, you are well tuned now!
 But I'll set down the pegs that make this music,
 As honest as I am.

Othello.   Come, let us to the castle.
 News, friends, our wars are done, the Turks are drown'd.

How does my old acquaintance of this isle?
Honey, you shall be well desired in Cyprus;
I have found great love amongst them. O my sweet,
I prattle out of fashion, and I dote
In mine own comforts. I prithee, good Iago,
Go to the bay and disembark my coffers.
Bring thou the master to the citadel;
He is a good one, and his worthiness
Does challenge much respect. Come, Desdemona,
Once more well met at Cyprus.

Exeunt all but Iago *and* Roderigo.

Iago. Do thou meet me presently at the harbour. Come hither.
If thou be'st valiant—as, they say, base men being in love
have then a nobility in their natures more than is native to
them—list me. The lieutenant tonight watches on the court
of guard. First, I must tell thee this: Desdemona is directly in
love with him.

Roderigo. With him! Why, 'tis not possible.

Iago. Lay thy finger thus, and let thy soul be instructed. Mark me
with what violence she first loved the Moor, but for bragging
and telling her fantastical lies—and will she love him still for
prating? Let not thy discreet heart think it. Her eye must be
fed, and what delight shall she have to look on the devil?
When the blood is made dull with the act of sport, there
should be, again to inflame it and to give satiety a fresh
appetite, loveliness in favour, sympathy in years, manners and
beauties, all which the Moor is defective in. Now, for want of
these required conveniences, her delicate tenderness will find
itself abused, begin to heave the gorge, disrelish and abhor the
Moor; very nature will instruct her in it and compel her to
some second choice. Now sir, this granted—as it is a most
pregnant and unforced position—who stands so eminent in

the degree of this fortune as Cassio does? A knave very
voluble, no further conscionable than in putting on the mere
form of civil and humane seeming, for the better compassing
of his salt and most hidden loose affection? Why none, why
none: a slipper and subtle knave, a finder out of occasions, that
has an eye can stamp and counterfeit advantages, though true
advantage never present itself: a devilish knave! Besides, the
knave is handsome, young, and hath all those requisites in him
that folly and green minds look after. A pestilent complete
knave, and the woman hath found him already.

Roderigo. I cannot believe that in her; she's full of most blest
condition.

Iago. Blest fig's-end! The wine she drinks is made of grapes. If
she had been blest, she would never have loved the Moor:
blest pudding! Didst thou not see her paddle with the palm
of his hand? Didst not mark that?

Roderigo. Yes, that I did, but that was but courtesy.

Iago. Lechery, by this hand: an index and obscure prologue to the
history of lust and foul thoughts. They met so near with their
lips that their breaths embraced together. Villanous thoughts,
Roderigo! When these mutualities so marshal the way, hard at
hand comes the master and main exercise, th' incorporate
conclusion. Pish! But, sir, be you ruled by me. I have brought
you from Venice. Watch you tonight. For the command, I'll
lay't upon you: Cassio knows you not. I'll not be far from you;
do you find some occasion to anger Cassio, either by speaking
too loud or tainting his discipline, or from what other course
you please which the time shall more favourably minister.

Roderigo. Well.

Iago. Sir, he is rash and very sudden in choler, and haply may
strike at you: provoke him, that he may, for even out of that

will I cause these of Cyprus to mutiny, whose qualification shall come into no true taste again but by the displanting of Cassio. So shall you have a shorter journey to your desires, by the means I shall then have to prefer them and the impediment most profitably removed, without the which there were no expectation of our prosperity.

Roderigo. I will do this, if I can bring it to any opportunity.

Iago. I warrant thee. Meet me by and by at the citadel: I must fetch his necessaries ashore. Farewell.

Roderigo. Adieu.

Exit.

Iago. That Cassio loves her, I do well believe it;
That she loves him, 'tis apt and of great credit.
The Moor, howbeit that I endure him not,
Is of a constant, loving, noble nature,
And I dare think he'll prove to Desdemona
A most dear husband. Now I do love her too,
Not out of absolute lust, though peradventure
I stand accountant for as great a sin,
But partly led to diet my revenge,
For that I do suspect the lusty Moor
Hath leap'd into my seat, the thought whereof
Doth like a poisonous mineral gnaw my inwards;
And nothing can or shall content my soul
Till I am even'd with him, wife for wife;
Or failing so, yet that I put the Moor
At least into a jealousy so strong
That judgement cannot cure. Which thing to do,
If this poor trash of Venice, whom I trash
For his quick hunting, stand the putting on,
I'll have our Michael Cassio on the hip,
Abuse him to the Moor in the rank garb—

For I fear Cassio with my night-cap too—
Make the Moor thank me, love me and reward me,
For making him egregiously an ass
And practising upon his peace and quiet
Even to madness. 'Tis here, but yet confused:
Knavery's plain face is never seen till used.

Exit.

scene 2. [*A street*]

Enter a Herald *with a proclamation; People following*

Herald. It is Othello's pleasure, our noble and valiant general, that upon certain tidings now arrived, importing the mere perdition of the Turkish fleet, every man put himself into triumph: some to dance, some to make bonfires, each man to what sport and revels his addiction leads him. For, besides these beneficial news, it is the celebration of his nuptial. So much was his pleasure should be proclaimed. All offices are open, and there is full liberty of feasting from this present hour of five till the bell have told eleven. Heaven bless the isle of Cyprus and our noble general Othello!

Exeunt.

scene 3. [*A hall in the castle*]

Enter Othello, Desdemona, Cassio, *and* Attendants

Othello. Good Michael, look you to the guard tonight.
Let's teach ourselves that honourable stop,
Not to outsport discretion.

Cassio. Iago hath direction what to do,
But notwithstanding with my personal eye
Will I look to't.

Othello.　　　　Iago is most honest.
　Michael, good night. Tomorrow with your earliest
　Let me have speech with you. Come, my dear love,
　The purchase made, the fruits are to ensue;
　That profit's yet to come 'tween me and you.
　Good night

　　　　　　　　　Exeunt Othello, Desdemona, *and* Attendants.

　　　　　　　　　　　Enter Iago

Cassio. Welcome, Iago; we must to the watch.

Iago. Not this hour, lieutenant, 'tis not yet ten o' th' clock. Our general cast us thus early for the love of his Desdemona, who let us not therefore blame; he hath not yet made wanton the night with her, and she is sport for Jove.

Cassio. She's a most exquisite lady.

Iago. And, I'll warrant her, full of game.

Cassio. Indeed she's a most fresh and delicate creature.

Iago. What an eye she has! Methinks it sounds a parley to provocation.

Cassio. An inviting eye; and yet methinks right modest.

Iago. And when she speaks, is it not an alarum to love?

Cassio. She is indeed perfection.

Iago. Well, happiness to their sheets! Come, lieutenant, I have a stoup of wine, and here without are a brace of Cyprus gallants that would fain have a measure to the health of black Othello.

Cassio. Not tonight, good Iago, I have very poor and unhappy brains for drinking. I could well wish courtesy would invent some other custom of entertainment.

Iago. O, they are our friends. But one cup: I'll drink for you.

Cassio. I have drunk but one cup tonight, and that was craftily qualified too, and behold what innovation it makes here: I am unfortunate in the infirmity, and dare not task my weakness with any more.

Iago. What, man! 'tis a night of revels, the gallants desire it.

Cassio. Where are they?

Iago. Here at the door; I pray you, call them in.

Cassio. I'll do't; but it dislikes me.

Exit.

Iago. If I can fasten but one cup upon him,
With that which he hath drunk tonight already,
He'll be as full of quarrel and offence
As my young mistress' dog. Now my sick fool Roderigo,
Whom love hath turn'd almost the wrong side out,
To Desdemona hath tonight caroused
Potations pottle-deep, and he's to watch.
Three lads of Cyprus, noble swelling spirits
That hold their honours in a wary distance,
The very elements of this warlike isle,
Have I tonight fluster'd with flowing cups,
And they watch too. Now, 'mongst this flock of drunkards,
Am I to put our Cassio in some action
That may offend the isle. But here they come:
If consequence do but approve my dream,
My boat sails freely, both with wind and stream.

Re-enter Cassio; *with him* Montano *and* Gentlemen;
Servants following with wine

Cassio. 'Fore God, they have given me a rouse already.

Montano. Good faith, a little one, not past a pint, as I am a soldier.

Iago. Some wine, ho!

[*Sings*]

And let me the canakin clink, clink,
And let me the canakin clink:
A soldier's a man,
A life's but a span,
Why then let a soldier drink.

Some wine, boys!

Cassio. 'Fore God, an excellent song.

Iago. I learned it in England, where indeed they are most potent in potting: your Dane, your German, and your swag-bellied Hollander—Drink, ho!—are nothing to your English.

Cassio. Is your Englishman so expert in his drinking?

Iago. Why, he drinks you with facility your Dane dead drunk; he sweats not to overthrow your Almain; he gives your Hollander a vomit ere the next pottle can be filled.

Cassio. To the health of our general!

Montano. I am for it, lieutenant, and I'll do you justice.

Iago. O sweet England!

[*Sings*]

King Stephen was a worthy peer,
His breeches cost him but a crown;
He held them sixpence all too dear,
With that he call'd the tailor lown.

He was a wight of high renown,
And thou art but of low degree.
'Tis pride that pulls the country down,
Then take thine auld cloak about thee.

Some wine, ho!

Cassio. Why, this is a more exquisite song than the other.

Iago. Will you hear't again?

Cassio. No, for I hold him to be unworthy of his place that does those things. Well, God's above all, and there be souls must be saved, and there be souls must not be saved.

Iago. It's true, good lieutenant.

Cassio. For mine own part—no offence to the general, nor any man of quality—I hope to be saved.

Iago. And so do I too, lieutenant.

Cassio. Ay, but, by your leave, not before me; the lieutenant is to be saved before the ancient. Let's have no more of this, let's to our affairs. God forgive us our sins! Gentlemen, let's look to our business. Do not think, gentlemen, I am drunk: this is my ancient, this is my right hand, and this is my left. I am not drunk now; I can stand well enough, and speak well enough.

All. Excellent well.

Cassio. Why, very well then; you must not think then that I am drunk.

Exit.

Montano. To the platform, masters; come, let's set the watch.

Iago. You see this fellow that is gone before,
    He is a soldier fit to stand by Cæasar
    And give direction. And do but see his vice,
    'Tis to his virtue a just equinox,
    The one as long as th' other: 'tis pity of him.
    I fear the trust Othello puts him in
    On some odd time of his infirmity
    Will shake this island.

Montano.   But is he often thus?

Iago. 'Tis evermore the prologue to his sleep:
    He'll watch the horologe a double set,
    If drink rock not his cradle.

Montano.   It were well
  The general were put in mind of it.
  Perhaps he sees it not, or his good nature
  Prizes the virtue that appears in Cassio
  And looks not on his evils: is not this true?

                              Enter Roderigo

Iago. [*Aside to him*] How now, Roderigo!
  I pray you, after the lieutenant, go.

                                        Exit Roderigo.

Montano. And 'tis great pity that the noble Moor
  Should hazard such a place as his own second
  With one of an ingraft infirmity.
  It were an honest action to say
  So to the Moor.

Iago.   Not I, for this fair island.
  I do love Cassio well, and would do much
  To cure him of this evil:—But hark! What noise?

                              A cry within: "Help! help!"

                    Re-enter Cassio, *driving in* Roderigo

Cassio. 'Zounds! You rogue! You rascal!

Montano. What's the matter, lieutenant?

Cassio. A knave teach me my duty? But I'll beat the knave into
  a wicker bottle.

Roderigo. Beat me!

Cassio. Dost thou prate, rogue?

                                        Striking Roderigo.

Montano. Nay, good lieutenant! I pray you, sir, hold your hand.

Cassio. Let me go, sir, or I'll knock you o'er the mazzard.

Montano. Come, come, you're drunk.

Cassio. Drunk!

                                                    They fight.

Iago. [*Aside to* Roderigo] Away, I say, go out, and cry a mutiny.

                                        Exit Roderigo.

   Nay, good lieutenant! God's will, gentlemen!
   Help, ho!—Lieutenant—sir—Montano—sir—
   Help, masters!—Here's a goodly watch indeed!

                                        A bell rings.

   Who's that which rings the bell?—Diablo, ho!
   The town will rise: God's will, lieutenant, hold;
   You will be shamed for ever.

                    Re-enter Othello *and* Attendants

Othello. What is the matter here?

Montano. 'Zounds, I bleed still;
   I am hurt to the death: he dies!

                                        Charges Cassio.

Othello. Hold, for your lives!

Iago. Hold, ho! Lieutenant—sir—Montano—gentlemen—
   Have you forgot all sense of place and duty?
   Hold! The general speaks to you; hold, hold, for shame!

Othello. Why, how now, ho! From whence ariseth this?
   Are we turn'd Turks, and to ourselves do that
   Which heaven hath forbid the Ottomites?
   For Christian shame, put by this barbarous brawl:
   He that stirs next to carve for his own rage
   Holds his soul light; he dies upon his motion.
   Silence that dreadful bell. It frights the isle
   From her propriety. What is the matter, masters?
   Honest Iago, that look'st dead with grieving,
   Speak, who began this? On thy love, I charge thee.

Iago. I do not know, friends all, but now, even now,
   In quarter and in terms like bride and groom
   Devesting them for bed; and then, but now,
   As if some planet had unwitted men,

Swords out, and tilting one at other's breast
In opposition bloody. I cannot speak
Any beginning to this peevish odds,
And would in action glorious I had lost
Those legs that brought me to a part of it!

Othello. How comes it, Michael, you are thus forgot?

Cassio. I pray you, pardon me; I cannot speak.

Othello. Worthy Montano, you were wont be civil;
The gravity and stillness of your youth
The world hath noted, and your name is great
In mouths of wisest censure. What's the matter
That you unlace your reputation thus,
And spend your rich opinion for the name
Of a night-brawler? Give me answer to it.

Montano. Worthy Othello, I am hurt to danger:
Your officer, Iago, can inform you—
While I spare speech, which something now offends me—
Of all that I do know. Nor know I aught
By me that's said or done amiss this night
Unless self-charity be sometimes a vice,
And to defend ourselves it be a sin
When violence assails us.

Othello.   Now, by heaven,
My blood begins my safer guides to rule,
And passion, having my best judgement collied,
Assays to lead the way. If I once stir,
Or do but lift this arm, the best of you
Shall sink in my rebuke. Give me to know
How this foul rout began, who set it on,
And he that is approved in this offence,
Though he had twinn'd with me, both at a birth,
Shall lose me. What! In a town of war,

Yet wild, the people's hearts brimful of fear,
To manage private and domestic quarrel?
In night, and on the court and guard of safety!
'Tis monstrous. Iago, who began't?

Montano. If partially affined or leagued in office
  Thou dost deliver more or less than truth,
  Thou art no soldier.

Iago.   Touch me not so near:
  I had rather have this tongue cut from my mouth
  Than it should do offence to Michael Cassio,
  Yet I persuade myself to speak the truth
  Shall nothing wrong him. Thus it is, general.
  Montano and myself being in speech,
  There comes a fellow crying out for help,
  And Cassio following him with determined sword
  To execute upon him. Sir, this gentleman
  Steps in to Cassio and entreats his pause;
  Myself the crying fellow did pursue,
  Lest by his clamour—as it so fell out—
  The town might fall in fright. He, swift of foot,
  Outran my purpose, and I return'd the rather
  For that I heard the clink and fall of swords
  And Cassio high in oath, which till tonight
  I ne'er might say before. When I came back—
  For this was brief—I found them close together,
  At blow and thrust, even as again they were
  When you yourself did part them.
  More of this matter cannot I report.
  But men are men; the best sometimes forget.
  Though Cassio did some little wrong to him,
  As men in rage strike those that wish them best,
  Yet surely Cassio, I believe, received

From him that fled some strange indignity,
Which patience could not pass.

Othello.   I know, Iago,
Thy honesty and love doth mince this matter,
Making it light to Cassio. Cassio, I love thee,
But never more be officer of mine.

                         Re-enter Desdemona, *attended.*
Look if my gentle love be not raised up!
I'll make thee an example.

Desdemona.   What's the matter?

Othello. All's well now, sweeting, come away to bed.
Sir, for your hurts, myself will be your surgeon.

                              To Montano, *who is led off.*
Lead him off.
Iago, look with care about the town
And silence those whom this vile brawl distracted.
Come, Desdemona: 'tis the soldiers' life
To have their balmy slumbers waked with strife.

                              Exeunt all but Iago *and* Cassio.

Iago. What, are you hurt, lieutenant?

Cassio. Ay, past all surgery.

Iago. Marry, God forbid!

Cassio. Reputation, reputation, reputation! O, I have lost my
reputation! I have lost the immortal part of myself, and what
remains is bestial. My reputation, Iago, my reputation!

Iago. As I am an honest man, I thought you had received some
bodily wound; there is more sense in that than in reputation.
Reputation is an idle and most false imposition, oft got
without merit and lost without deserving. You have lost no
reputation at all, unless you repute yourself such a loser.
What, man! There are ways to recover the general again: you

are but now cast in his mood, a punishment more in policy
than in malice, even so as one would beat his offenceless dog
to affright an imperious lion. Sue to him again, and he's
yours.

Cassio. I will rather sue to be despised than to deceive so good a
commander with so slight, so drunken, and so indiscreet an
officer. Drunk? And speak parrot? And squabble? Swagger?
Swear? And discourse fustian with one's own shadow?
O thou invisible spirit of wine, if thou hast no name to be
known by, let us call thee devil!

Iago. What was he that you followed with your sword? What
had he done to you?

Cassio. I know not.

Iago. Is't possible?

Cassio. I remember a mass of things, but nothing distinctly;
a quarrel, but nothing wherefore. O God, that men should
put an enemy in their mouths to steal away their brains! That
we should, with joy, pleasance, revel and applause, transform
ourselves into beasts!

Iago. Why, but you are now well enough: how came you thus
recovered?

Cassio. It hath pleased the devil drunkenness to give place to the
devil wrath. One unperfectness shows me another, to make
me frankly despise myself.

Iago. Come, you are too severe a moraler. As the time, the place,
and the condition of this country stands, I could heartily
wish this had not befallen, but since it is as it is, mend it for
your own good.

Cassio. I will ask him for my place again; he shall tell me I am a
drunkard! Had I as many mouths as Hydra, such an answer
would stop them all. To be now a sensible man, by and by a

fool, and presently a beast! O strange! Every inordinate cup is unblest, and the ingredient is a devil.

Iago. Come, come, good wine is a good familiar creature, if it be well used: exclaim no more against it. And, good lieutenant, I think you think I love you.

Cassio. I have well approved it, sir. I drunk!

Iago. You or any man living may be drunk at some time, man. I'll tell you what you shall do. Our general's wife is now the general. I may say so in this respect, for that he hath devoted and given up himself to the contemplation, mark and denotement of her parts and graces. Confess yourself freely to her, importune her help to put you in your place again. She is of so free, so kind, so apt, so blessed a disposition, she holds it a vice in her goodness not to do more than she is requested. This broken joint between you and her husband entreat her to splinter, and, my fortunes against any lay worth naming, this crack of your love shall grow stronger than it was before.

Cassio. You advise me well.

Iago. I protest, in the sincerity of love and honest kindness.

Cassio. I think it freely, and betimes in the morning I will beseech the virtuous Desdemona to undertake for me. I am desperate of my fortunes if they check me here.

Iago. You are in the right. Good night, lieutenant, I must to the watch.

Cassio. Good night, honest Iago.

Exit.

Iago. And what's he then that says I play the villain?
    When this advice is free I give and honest,
    Probal to thinking, and indeed the course
    To win the Moor again? For 'tis most easy
    Th' inclining Desdemona to subdue

In any honest suit. She's framed as fruitful
As the free elements. And then for her
To win the Moor, were't to renounce his baptism,
All seals and symbols of redeemed sin,
His soul is so enfetter'd to her love
That she may make, unmake, do what she list,
Even as her appetite shall play the god
With his weak function. How am I then a villain
To counsel Cassio to this parallel course,
Directly to his good? Divinity of hell!
When devils will the blackest sins put on,
They do suggest at first with heavenly shows,
As I do now. For whiles this honest fool
Plies Desdemona to repair his fortunes,
And she for him pleads strongly to the Moor,
I'll pour this pestilence into his ear,
That she repeals him for her body's lust.
And by how much she strives to do him good,
She shall undo her credit with the Moor.
So will I turn her virtue into pitch,
And out of her own goodness make the net
That shall enmesh them all.

Enter Roderigo

How now, Roderigo!

Roderigo. I do follow here in the chase not like a hound that
hunts, but one that fills up the cry. My money is almost
spent, I have been tonight exceedingly well cudgelled, and
I think the issue will be I shall have so much experience for
my pains. And so, with no money at all and a little more wit,
return again to Venice.

Iago. How poor are they that have not patience!
What wound did ever heal but by degrees?

Thou know'st we work by wit and not by witchcraft,
And wit depends on dilatory time.
Does't not go well? Cassio hath beaten thee,
And thou by that small hurt hast cashier'd Cassio.
Though other things grow fair against the sun,
Yet fruits that blossom first will first be ripe:
Content thyself awhile. By the mass, 'tis morning;
Pleasure and action make the hours seem short.
Retire thee, go where thou art billeted,
Away, I say, thou shalt know more hereafter:
Nay, get thee gone.

Exit Roderigo.

Two things are to be done:
My wife must move for Cassio to her mistress;
I'll set her on.
Myself the while to draw the Moor apart
And bring him jump when he may Cassio find
Soliciting his wife: ay, that's the way!
Dull not device by coldness and delay.

Exit.

act 3

scene 1. [*Before the castle*]

Enter Cassio *and some* Musicians

Cassio. Masters, play here, I will content your pains;
Something that's brief, and bid 'Good morrow, general.'

Music.

Enter Clown

Clown. Why, masters, have your instruments been in Naples,
that they speak i' the nose thus?

First Musician. How, sir, how?

Clown. Are these, I pray you, wind instruments?

First Musician. Ay marry are they, sir.

Clown. O, thereby hangs a tail.

First Musician. Whereby hangs a tale, sir?

Clown. Marry, sir, by many a wind instrument that I know. But,
masters, here's money for you, and the general so likes your
music that he desires you, for love's sake, to make no more
noise with it.

First Musician. Well, sir, we will not.

Clown. If you have any music that may not be heard, to't again.
   But, as they say, to hear music the general does not greatly care.

First Musician. We have none such, sir.

Clown. Then put up your pipes in your bag, for I'll away. Go,
   vanish into air, away!

Exeunt Musicians.

Cassio. Dost thou hear, my honest friend?

Clown. No, I hear not your honest friend; I hear you.

Cassio. Prithee, keep up thy quillets. There's a poor piece of
   gold for thee. If the gentlewoman that attends the general's
   wife be stirring, tell her there's one Cassio entreats her a little
   favour of speech: wilt thou do this?

Clown. She is stirring, sir. If she will stir hither, I shall seem to
   notify unto her.

Cassio. Do, good my friend.

Exit Clown.

Enter Iago
In happy time, Iago.

Iago. You have not been a-bed, then?

Cassio. Why, no, the day had broke
   Before we parted. I have made bold, Iago,
   To send in to your wife: my suit to her
   Is that she will to virtuous Desdemona
   Procure me some access.

Iago.   I'll send her to you presently,
   And I'll devise a mean to draw the Moor
   Out of the way, that your converse and business
   May be more free.

Cassio. I humbly thank you for't.

Exit Iago.

I never knew
A Florentine more kind and honest.

                Enter Emilia

Emilia. Good morrow, good lieutenant. I am sorry
  For your displeasure, but all will sure be well.
  The general and his wife are talking of it,
  And she speaks for you stoutly: the Moor replies
  That he you hurt is of great fame in Cyprus
  And great affinity, and that in wholesome wisdom
  He might not but refuse you; but he protests he loves you,
  And needs no other suitor but his likings
  To take the safest occasion by the front
  To bring you in again.

Cassio.   Yet I beseech you,
  If you think fit, or that it may be done,
  Give me advantage of some brief discourse
  With Desdemona alone.

Emilia.   Pray you, come in:
  I will bestow you where you shall have time
  To speak your bosom freely.

Cassio.   I am much bound to you.

                       Exeunt.

scene 2. [*A room in the castle*]

        Enter Othello, Iago, *and* Gentlemen

Othello. These letters give, Iago, to the pilot,
  And by him do my duties to the senate.
  That done, I will be walking on the works;
  Repair there to me.

Iago.   Well, my good lord, I'll do't.

Othello. This fortification, gentlemen, shall we see't?

Gentlemen. We'll wait upon your lordship.

Exeunt.

scene 3. [*The garden of the castle*]

Enter Desdemona, Cassio, *and* Emilia

Desdemona. Be thou assured, good Cassio, I will do
　　All my abilities in thy behalf.

Emilia. Good madam, do: I warrant it grieves my husband
　　As if the case were his.

Desdemona. O, that's an honest fellow. Do not doubt, Cassio,
　　But I will have my lord and you again
　　As friendly as you were.

Cassio.　　　　　　　　Bounteous madam,
　　Whatever shall become of Michael Cassio,
　　He's never anything but your true servant.

Desdemona. I know't, I thank you. You do love my lord,
　　You have known him long, and be you well assured
　　He shall in strangeness stand no farther off
　　Than in a politic distance.

Cassio.　　　　　　　Ay, but, lady,
　　That policy may either last so long,
　　Or feed upon such nice and waterish diet,
　　Or breed itself so out of circumstance,
　　That, I being absent and my place supplied,
　　My general will forget my love and service.

Desdemona. Do not doubt that; before Emilia here
　　I give thee warrant of thy place. Assure thee,
　　If I do vow a friendship, I'll perform it

To the last article. My lord shall never rest;
I'll watch him tame and talk him out of patience,
His bed shall seem a school, his board a shrift,
I'll intermingle everything he does
With Cassio's suit: therefore be merry, Cassio,
For thy solicitor shall rather die
Than give thy cause away.

Enter Othello *and* Iago, *at a distance*

Emilia. Madam, here comes my lord.

Cassio. Madam, I'll take my leave.

Desdemona. Nay, stay and hear me speak.

Cassio. Madam, not now. I am very ill at ease, Unfit for mine
own purposes.

Desdemona. Well, do your discretion.

Exit Cassio.

Iago. Ha! I like not that.

Othello. What dost thou say?

Iago. Nothing, my lord; or if—I know not what.

Othello. Was not that Cassio parted from my wife?

Iago. Cassio, my lord! No, sure, I cannot think it
That he would steal away so guilty-like,
Seeing you coming.

Othello.   I do believe 'twas he.

Desdemona. How now, my lord!
I have been talking with a suitor here,
A man that languishes in your displeasure.

Othello. Who is't you mean?

Desdemona. Why, your lieutenant, Cassio. Good my lord,
If I have any grace or power to move you,

His present reconciliation take,
For if he be not one that truly loves you,
That errs in ignorance and not in cunning,
I have no judgement in an honest face.
I prithee, call him back.

Othello. Went he hence now?

Desdemona. Ay, sooth, so humbled
That he hath left part of his grief with me,
To suffer with him. Good love, call him back.

Othello. Not now, sweet Desdemon; some other time.

Desdemona. But shall't be shortly?

Othello. The sooner, sweet, for you.

Desdemona. Shall't be tonight at supper?

Othello. No, not tonight.

Desdemona. Tomorrow dinner then?

Othello. I shall not dine at home;
I meet the captains at the citadel.

Desdemona. Why then tomorrow night, or Tuesday morn;
On Tuesday noon, or night; on Wednesday morn.
I prithee name the time, but let it not
Exceed three days: in faith, he's penitent,
And yet his trespass, in our common reason—
Save that, they say, the wars must make examples
Out of their best—is not almost a fault
To incur a private check. When shall he come?
Tell me, Othello. I wonder in my soul
What you would ask me, that I should deny
Or stand so mammering on. What! Michael Cassio
That came a-wooing with you, and so many a time
When I have spoke of you dispraisingly

Hath ta'en your part, to have so much to do
To bring him in, Trust me, I could do much—

Othello. Prithee, no more. Let him come when he will;
I will deny thee nothing.

Desdemona.   Why, this is not a boon.
'Tis as I should entreat you wear your gloves,
Or feed on nourishing dishes, or keep you warm,
Or sue to you to do a peculiar profit
To your own person. Nay, when I have a suit
Wherein I mean to touch your love indeed,
It shall be full of poise and difficult weight,
And fearful to be granted.

Othello.   I will deny thee nothing,
Whereon, I do beseech thee, grant me this,
To leave me but a little to myself.

Desdemona. Shall I deny you? No, farewell, my lord.

Othello. Farewell, my Desdemona, I'll come to thee straight.

Desdemona. Emilia, come.
[*To Othello*] Be as your fancies teach you.
Whate'er you be, I am obedient.
                              Exeunt Desdemona *and* Emilia.

Othello. Excellent wretch! Perdition catch my soul
But I do love thee! And when I love thee not,
Chaos is come again.

Iago. My noble lord—

Othello.   What dost thou say, Iago?

Iago. Did Michael Cassio, when you woo'd my lady,
Know of your love?

Othello. He did, from first to last: why dost thou ask?

Iago. But for a satisfaction of my thought,
  No further harm.

Othello.   Why of thy thought, Iago?

Iago. I did not think he had been acquainted with her.

Othello. O, yes, and went between us very oft.

Iago. Indeed!

Othello. Indeed? Ay, indeed. Discern'st thou aught in that?
  Is he not honest?

Iago. Honest, my lord?

Othello. Honest! Ay, honest.

Iago. My lord, for aught I know.

Othello. What dost thou think?

Iago. Think, my lord?

Othello. Think, my lord! By heaven, he echoes me
  As if there were some monster in his thought
  Too hideous to be shown. Thou dost mean something:
  I heard thee say even now, thou likedst not that,
  When Cassio left my wife. What didst not like?
  And when I told thee he was of my counsel
  In my whole course of wooing, thou criedst 'Indeed!'
  And didst contract and purse thy brow together,
  As if thou then hadst shut up in thy brain
  Some horrible conceit. If thou dost love me,
  Show me thy thought.

Iago. My lord, you know I love you.

Othello.   I think thou dost.
  And for I know thou'rt full of love and honesty
  And weigh'st thy words before thou givest them breath,
  Therefore these stops of thine fright me the more.

For such things in a false disloyal knave
Are tricks of custom, but in a man that's just
They're close delations, working from the heart,
That passion cannot rule.

Iago.   For Michael Cassio,
  I dare be sworn I think that he is honest.

Othello. I think so too.

Iago.   Men should be what they seem,
  Or those that be not, would they might seem none!

Othello. Certain men should be what they seem.

Iago. Why then I think Cassio's an honest man.

Othello. Nay, yet there's more in this:
  I prithee, speak to me as to thy thinkings,
  As thou dost ruminate, and give thy worst of thoughts
  The worst of words.

Iago.   Good my lord, pardon me:
  Though I am bound to every act of duty,
  I am not bound to that all slaves are free to.
  Utter my thoughts? Why, say they are vile and false;
  As where's that palace whereinto foul things
  Sometimes intrude not? Who has a breast so pure,
  But some uncleanly apprehensions
  Keep leets and law-days, and in session sit
  With meditations lawful?

Othello. Thou dost conspire against thy friend, Iago,
  If thou but think'st him wrong'd and makest his ear
  A stranger to thy thoughts.

Iago.   I do beseech you—
  Though I perchance am vicious in my guess,
  As I confess it is my nature's plague

To spy into abuses, and oft my jealousy
Shapes faults that are not—that your wisdom
From one that so imperfectly conceits
Would take no notice, nor build yourself a trouble
Out of his scattering and unsure observance.
It were not for your quiet nor your good,
Nor for my manhood, honesty, or wisdom,
To let you know my thoughts.

Othello.   What dost thou mean?

Iago. Good name in man and woman, dear my lord,
Is the immediate jewel of their souls:
Who steals my purse steals trash; 'tis something, nothing.
'Twas mine, 'tis his, and has been slave to thousands.
But he that filches from me my good name
Robs me of that which not enriches him
And makes me poor indeed.

Othello. By heaven, I'll know thy thoughts.

Iago. You cannot, if my heart were in your hand;
Nor shall not, whilst 'tis in my custody.

Othello. Ha!

Iago.   O beware, my lord, of jealousy!
It is the green-eyed monster, which doth mock
The meat it feeds on. That cuckold lives in bliss
Who, certain of his fate, loves not his wronger,
But O, what damned minutes tells he o'er
Who dotes yet doubts, suspects yet strongly loves!

Othello. O misery!

Iago. Poor and content is rich, and rich enough;
But riches fineless is as poor as winter
To him that ever fears he shall be poor.

Good God, the souls of all my tribe defend
From jealousy!

Othello.   Why, why is this?
Think'st thou I 'ld make a life of jealousy,
To follow still the changes of the moon
With fresh suspicions? No, to be once in doubt
Is once to be resolved. Exchange me for a goat
When I shall turn the business of my soul
To such exsufflicate and blown surmises,
Matching thy inference. 'Tis not to make me jealous
To say my wife is fair, feeds well, loves company,
Is free of speech, sings, plays and dances well;
Where virtue is, these are more virtuous.
Nor from mine own weak merits will I draw
The smallest fear or doubt of her revolt,
For she had eyes, and chose me. No, Iago,
I'll see before I doubt; when I doubt, prove;
And on the proof, there is no more but this,
Away at once with love or jealousy!

Iago. I am glad of it, for now I shall have reason
To show the love and duty that I bear you
With franker spirit: therefore, as I am bound,
Receive it from me. I speak not yet of proof.
Look to your wife: observe her well with Cassio.
Wear your eye thus, not jealous nor secure.
I would not have your free and noble nature
Out of self-bounty be abused; look to't.
I know our country disposition well;
In Venice they do let heaven see the pranks
They dare not show their husbands. Their best conscience
Is not to leave't undone, but keep't unknown.

Othello. Dost thou say so?

Iago. She did deceive her father, marrying you,
   And when she seem'd to shake and fear your looks,
   She loved them most.

Othello.   And so she did.

Iago.   Why, go to then.
   She that so young could give out such a seeming,
   To seel her father's eyes up close as oak—
   He thought 'twas witchcraft—but I am much to blame.
   I humbly do beseech you of your pardon
   For too much loving you.

Othello.   I am bound to thee for ever.

Iago. I see this hath a little dash'd your spirits.

Othello. Not a jot, not a jot.

Iago.   I' faith, I fear it has.
   I hope you will consider what is spoke
   Comes from my love. But I do see you 're moved:
   I am to pray you not to strain my speech
   To grosser issues nor to larger reach
   Than to suspicion.

Othello. I will not.

Iago.   Should you do so, my lord,
   My speech should fall into such vile success
   As my thoughts aim not at. Cassio's my worthy friend—
   My lord, I see you're moved.

Othello.   No, not much moved.
   I do not think but Desdemona's honest.

Iago. Long live she so! And long live you to think so.

Othello. And yet, how nature erring from itself—

Iago. Ay, there's the point: as—to be bold with you—
    Not to affect many proposed matches
    Of her own clime, complexion and degree,
    Whereto we see in all things nature tends—
    Foh! One may smell in such a will most rank,
    Foul disproportion, thoughts unnatural.
    But pardon me: I do not in position
    Distinctly speak of her, though I may fear
    Her will, recoiling to her better judgement,
    May fall to match you with her country forms,
    And happily repent.

Othello.   Farewell, farewell.
    If more thou dost perceive, let me know more;
    Set on thy wife to observe. Leave me, Iago.

Iago. [*Going*] My lord, I take my leave.

Othello. Why did I marry? This honest creature doubtless
    Sees and knows more, much more, than he unfolds.

Iago. [*Returning*] My lord, I would I might entreat your honour
    To scan this thing no further. Leave it to time.
    Though it be fit that Cassio have his place,
    For sure he fills it up with great ability,
    Yet if you please to hold him off awhile,
    You shall by that perceive him and his means:
    Note if your lady strain his entertainment
    With any strong or vehement importunity;
    Much will be seen in that. In the meantime,
    Let me be thought too busy in my fears—
    As worthy cause I have to fear I am—
    And hold her free, I do beseech your honour.

Othello. Fear not my government.

Iago. I once more take my leave.

                                 Exit.

Othello. This fellow's of exceeding honesty
 And knows all qualities, with a learned spirit,
 Of human dealings. If I do prove her haggard,
 Though that her jesses were my dear heart-strings,
 I'd whistle her off and let her down the wind
 To prey at fortune. Haply, for I am black
 And have not those soft parts of conversation
 That chamberers have, or for I am declined
 Into the vale of years—yet that's not much—
 She's gone, I am abused, and my relief
 Must be to loathe her. O curse of marriage,
 That we can call these delicate creatures ours
 And not their appetites! I had rather be a toad
 And live upon the vapour of a dungeon,
 Than keep a corner in the thing I love
 For others' uses. Yet, 'tis the plague of great ones,
 Prerogatived are they less than the base;
 'Tis destiny unshunnable, like death,
 Even then this forked plague is fated to us
 When we do quicken. Desdemona comes:
    Re-enter Desdemona *and* Emilia
 If she be false, O then heaven mocks itself!
 I'll not believe't.

Desdemona.   How now, my dear Othello!
 Your dinner, and the generous islanders
 By you invited, do attend your presence.

Othello. I am to blame.

Desdemona.   Why do you speak so faintly?
 Are you not well?

Othello. I have a pain upon my forehead here.

Desdemona. Faith, that's with watching; 'twill away again.
Let me but bind it hard, within this hour
It will be well.

Othello.　　　　　Your napkin is too little.

　　　　　　He puts the handkerchief from him; and she drops it.

Let it alone. Come, I'll go in with you.

Desdemona. I am very sorry that you are not well.

　　　　　　　　　　Exeunt Othello *and* Desdemona.

Emilia. I am glad I have found this napkin:
This was her first remembrance from the Moor.
My wayward husband hath a hundred times
Woo'd me to steal it, but she so loves the token,
For he conjured her she should ever keep it,
That she reserves it evermore about her
To kiss and talk to. I'll have the work ta'en out
And give't Iago: what he will do with it
Heaven knows, not I.
I nothing but to please his fantasy.

　　　　　　　　　Re-enter Iago

Iago. How now! What do you here alone?

Emilia. Do not you chide; I have a thing for you.

Iago. A thing for me? It is a common thing—

Emilia. Ha!

Iago. To have a foolish wife.

Emilia. O, is that all? What will you give me now
For that same handkerchief?

Iago.　　　　　　　　What handkerchief?

Emilia. What handkerchief!
Why, that the Moor first gave to Desdemona,
That which so often you did bid me steal.

Iago. Hast stol'n it from her?

Emilia. No, faith, she let it drop by negligence
   And, to the advantage, I being here took 't up.
   Look, here it is.

Iago.   A good wench; give it me.

Emilia. What will you do with 't, that you have been so earnest
   To have me filch it?

Iago. [*Snatching it*] Why, what's that to you?

Emilia. If 't be not for some purpose of import,
   Give 't me again. Poor lady, she'll run mad
   When she shall lack it.

Iago. Be not acknown on 't; I have use for it.
   Go, leave me.

                                    Exit Emilia.

   I will in Cassio's lodging lose this napkin,
   And let him find it. Trifles light as air
   Are to the jealous confirmations strong
   As proofs of holy writ. This may do something.
   The Moor already changes with my poison:
   Dangerous conceits are in their natures poisons,
   Which at the first are scarce found to distaste,
   But with a little art upon the blood
   Burn like the mines of sulphur. I did say so:
   Look, where he comes!
                   Re-enter Othello
                   Not poppy nor mandragora,
   Nor all the drowsy syrups of the world,
   Shall ever medicine thee to that sweet sleep
   Which thou owedst yesterday.

Othello.   Ha! Ha! False to me?

Iago. Why, How now, general! No more of that.

Othello. Avaunt, be gone! Thou hast set me on the rack.
    I swear 'tis better to be much abused
    Than but to know't a little.

Iago.   How now, my lord!

Othello. What sense had I of her stol'n hours of lust?
    I saw 't not, thought it not, it harm'd not me:
    I slept the next night well, was free and merry;
    I found not Cassio's kisses on her lips.
    He that is robb'd, not wanting what is stol'n,
    Let him not know't and he's not robb'd at all.

Iago. I am sorry to hear this.

Othello. I had been happy if the general camp,
    Pioners and all, had tasted her sweet body,
    So I had nothing known. O, now forever
    Farewell the tranquil mind, farewell content!
    Farewell the plumed troop and the big wars
    That make ambition virtue! O farewell,
    Farewell the neighing steed and the shrill trump,
    The spirit-stirring drum, the ear-piercing fife,
    The royal banner and all quality,
    Pride, pomp and circumstance of glorious war!
    And, O you mortal engines whose rude throats
    The immortal Jove's dread clamours counterfeit,
    Farewell! Othello's occupation 's gone.

Iago. Is't possible, my lord?

Othello. Villain, be sure thou prove my love a whore;
    Be sure of it, give me the ocular proof,
    Or by the worth of man's eternal soul
    Thou hadst been better have been born a dog
    Than answer my waked wrath!

Iago.   Is't come to this?

Othello. Make me to see't, or at the least so prove it
   That the probation bear no hinge nor loop
   To hang a doubt on, or woe upon thy life!

Iago. My noble lord—

Othello. If thou dost slander her and torture me,
   Never pray more, abandon all remorse;
   On horror's head horrors accumulate;
   Do deeds to make heaven weep, all earth amazed,
   For nothing canst thou to damnation add
   Greater than that.

Iago.   O grace! O heaven defend me!
   Are you a man? Have you a soul or sense?
   God be wi' you, take mine office. O wretched fool,
   That livest to make thine honesty a vice!
   O monstrous world! Take note, take note, O world,
   To be direct and honest is not safe.
   I thank you for this profit, and from hence
   I'll love no friend sith love breeds such offence.

Othello. Nay, stay, thou shouldst be honest.

Iago. I should be wise; for honesty's a fool
   And loses that it works for.

Othello.   By the world,
   I think my wife be honest, and think she is not;
   I think that thou art just, and think thou art not.
   I'll have some proof. Her name, that was as fresh
   As Dian's visage, is now begrimed and black
   As mine own face. If there be cords or knives,
   Poison, or fire, or suffocating streams,
   I'll not endure it. Would I were satisfied!

Iago. I see, sir, you are eaten up with passion.
   I do repent me that I put it to you.
   You would be satisfied?

Othello.   Would! Nay, I will.

Iago. And may-but how? How satisfied, my lord?
   Would you, the supervisor, grossly gape on?
   Behold her topp'd?

Othello.   Death and damnation! O!

Iago. It were a tedious difficulty, I think,
   To bring them to that prospect. Damn them then,
   If ever mortal eyes do see them bolster
   More than their own! What then? How then?
   What shall I say? Where's satisfaction?
   It is impossible you should see this
   Were they as prime as goats, as hot as monkeys,
   As salt as wolves in pride, and fools as gross
   As ignorance made drunk. But yet, I say,
   If imputation and strong circumstances,
   Which lead directly to the door of truth,
   Will give you satisfaction, you may have't.

Othello. Give me a living reason she's disloyal.

Iago. I do not like the office.
   But sith I am enter'd in this cause so far,
   Prick'd to't by foolish honesty and love,
   I will go on. I lay with Cassio lately,
   And being troubled with a raging tooth,
   I could not sleep.
   There are a kind of men so loose of soul
   That in their sleeps will mutter their affairs:
   One of this kind is Cassio.
   In sleep I heard him say 'Sweet Desdemona,
   Let us be wary, let us hide our loves,'
   And then, sir, would he grip and wring my hand,
   Cry 'O sweet creature!' and then kiss me hard,
   As if he pluck'd up kisses by the roots

That grew upon my lips, then lay his leg
Over my thigh, and sigh and kiss, and then
Cry 'Cursed fate that gave thee to the Moor!'

Othello. O monstrous! Monstrous!

Iago.   Nay, this was but his dream.

Othello. But this denoted a foregone conclusion.
'Tis a shrewd doubt, though it be but a dream.

Iago. And this may help to thicken other proofs
That do demonstrate thinly.

Othello.   I'll tear her all to pieces.

Iago. Nay, but be wise, yet we see nothing done;
She may be honest yet. Tell me but this:
Have you not sometimes seen a handkerchief
Spotted with strawberries in your wife's hand?

Othello. I gave her such a one, 'twas my first gift.

Iago. I know not that, but such a handkerchief—
I am sure it was your wife's—did I today
See Cassio wipe his beard with.

Othello.   If it be that—

Iago. If it be that, or any that was hers,
It speaks against her with the other proofs.

Othello. O that the slave had forty thousand lives!
One is too poor, too weak for my revenge.
Now do I see 'tis true. Look here, Iago,
All my fond love thus do I blow to heaven:
'Tis gone.
Arise, black vengeance, from thy hollow hell!
Yield up, O love, thy crown and hearted throne
To tyrannous hate! Swell, bosom, with thy fraught,
For 'tis of aspics' tongues!

Iago. Yet be content.

Othello. O, blood, blood, blood!

Iago. Patience, I say, your mind perhaps may change.

Othello. Never, Iago. Like to the Pontic sea
 Whose icy current and compulsive course
 Ne'er feels retiring ebb, but keeps due on
 To the Propontic and the Hellespont,
 Even so my bloody thoughts with violent pace
 Shall ne'er look back, ne'er ebb to humble love,
 Till that a capable and wide revenge
 Swallow them up. Now by yond marble heaven,
 In the due reverence of a sacred vow

          Kneels.

 I here engage my words.

Iago.   Do not rise yet.

          Kneels.

 Witness, you ever-burning lights above,
 You elements that clip us round about,
 Witness that here Iago doth give up
 The execution of his wit, hands, heart,
 To wrong'd Othello's service! Let him command,
 And to obey shall be in me remorse
 What bloody business ever.

         They rise.

Othello.   I greet thy love,
 Not with vain thanks, but with acceptance bounteous,
 And will upon the instant put thee to 't.
 Within these three days let me hear thee say
 That Cassio's not alive.

Iago. My friend is dead; 'tis done at your request.
 But let her live.

Othello.   Damn her, lewd minx! O, damn her!
   Come, go with me apart; I will withdraw
   To furnish me with some swift means of death
   For the fair devil. Now art thou my lieutenant.

Iago. I am your own for ever.

                                                    Exeunt.

scene 4.   [*Before the castle*]

Enter Desdemona, Emilia, *and* Clown

Desdemona. Do you know, sirrah, where Lieutenant Cassio lies?

Clown. I dare not say he lies anywhere.

Desdemona. Why, man?

Clown. He's a soldier; and for one to say a soldier lies, is
   stabbing.

Desdemona. Go to, where lodges he?

Clown. To tell you where he lodges, is to tell you where I lie.

Desdemona. Can anything be made of this?

Clown. I know not where he lodges, and for me to devise a
   lodging, and say he lies here or he lies there, were to lie in
   mine own throat.

Desdemona. Can you inquire him out and be edified by report?

Clown. I will catechize the world for him, that is, make
   questions and by them answer.

Desdemona. Seek him, bid him come hither, tell him I have
   moved my lord on his behalf and hope all will be well.

Clown. To do this is within the compass of man's wit, and
   therefore I will attempt the doing it.

                                                    Exit.

Desdemona. Where should I lose that handkerchief, Emilia?

Emilia. I know not, madam.

Desdemona. Believe me, I had rather have lost my purse
　　Full of crusadoes, and but my noble Moor
　　Is true of mind and made of no such baseness
　　As jealous creatures are, it were enough
　　To put him to ill thinking.

Emilia. 　　　　　　　　Is he not jealous?

Desdemona. Who, he? I think the sun where he was born
　　Drew all such humours from him.

Emilia. 　　　　　　　　Look where he comes.

Desdemona. I will not leave him now till Cassio
　　Be call'd to him.
　　　　　　　　Enter Othello
　　　　　How is't with you, my lord?

Othello. Well, my good lady. [*Aside*] O, hardness to dissemble!
　　How do you, Desdemona?

Desdemona. 　　　　　　Well, my good lord.

Othello. Give me your hand. This hand is moist, my lady.

Desdemona. It yet has felt no age nor known no sorrow.

Othello. This argues fruitfulness and liberal heart:
　　Hot, hot, and moist. This hand of yours requires
　　A sequester from liberty, fasting and prayer,
　　Much castigation, exercise devout,
　　For here's a young and sweating devil here,
　　That commonly rebels. 'Tis a good hand,
　　A frank one.

Desdemona. 　　You may, indeed, say so,
　　For 'twas that hand that gave away my heart.

Othello. A liberal hand: the hearts of old gave hands,
    But our new heraldry is hands, not hearts.

Desdemona. I cannot speak of this. Come now, your promise.

Othello. What promise, chuck?

Desdemona. I have sent to bid Cassio come speak with you.

Othello. I have a salt and sorry rheum offends me.
    Lend me thy handkerchief.

Desdemona. Here, my lord.

Othello. That which I gave you.

Desdemona. I have it not about me.

Othello. Not?

Desdemona. No, indeed, my lord.

Othello. That's a fault. That handkerchief
    Did an Egyptian to my mother give;
    She was a charmer and could almost read
    The thoughts of people. she told her, while she kept it
    'Twould make her amiable and subdue my father
    Entirely to her love, but if she lost it
    Or made a gift of it, my father's eye
    Should hold her loathed and his spirits should hunt
    After new fancies. she dying gave it me
    And bid me, when my fate would have me wive,
    To give it her. I did so, and take heed on't,
    Make it a darling like your precious eye;
    To lose't or give't away were such perdition
    As nothing else could match.

Desdemona.   Is't possible?

Othello. 'Tis true: there's magic in the web of it.
    A sibyl, that had number'd in the world
    The sun to course two hundred compasses,

In her prophetic fury sew'd the work.
The worms were hallow'd that did breed the silk,
And it was dyed in mummy which the skilful
Conserved of maidens' hearts.

Desdemona.   Indeed! Is't true?

Othello. Most veritable, therefore look to't well.

Desdemona. Then would to God that I had never seen't!

Othello. Ha! Wherefore?

Desdemona. Why do you speak so startingly and rash?

Othello. Is't lost? Is't gone? Speak, is it out o' the way?

Desdemona. Heaven bless us!

Othello. Say you?

Desdemona. It is not lost, but what an if it were?

Othello. How!

Desdemona. I say, it is not lost.

Othello. Fetch't, let me see it.

Desdemona. Why, so I can, sir, but I will not now.
    This is a trick to put me from my suit.
    Pray you, let Cassio be received again.

Othello. Fetch me the handkerchief: my mind misgives.

Desdemona. Come, come,
    You'll never meet a more sufficient man.

Othello. The handkerchief!

Desdemona.   I pray, talk me of Cassio.

Othello. The handkerchief!

Desdemona.   A man that all his time
    Hath founded his good fortunes on your love,
    Shared dangers with you—

Othello. The handkerchief!

Desdemona. In faith, you are to blame.

Othello. 'zounds!

Exit.

Emilia. Is not this man jealous?

Desdemona. I ne'er saw this before.
Sure there's some wonder in this handkerchief;
I am most unhappy in the loss of it.

Emilia. 'Tis not a year or two shows us a man.
They are all but stomachs and we all but food:
They eat us hungerly, and when they are full
They belch us. Look you, Cassio and my husband.

Enter Cassio *and* Iago

Iago. There is no other way, 'tis she must do't,
And lo, the happiness! Go and importune her.

Desdemona. How now, good Cassio! What's the news with you?

Cassio. Madam, my former suit: I do beseech you
That by your virtuous means I may again
Exist, and be a member of his love
Whom I with all the office of my heart
Entirely honour. I would not be delay'd.
If my offence be of such mortal kind,
That nor my service past nor present sorrows
Nor purposed merit in futurity
Can ransom me into his love again,
But to know so must be my benefit;
So shall I clothe me in a forced content
And shut myself up in some other course
To fortune's alms.

Desdemona.   Alas, thrice-gentle Cassio!
My advocation is not now in tune;

My lord is not my lord, nor should I know him
Were he in favour as in humour alter'd.
So help me every spirit sanctified,
As I have spoken for you all my best
And stood within the blank of his displeasure
For my free speech! You must awhile be patient:
What I can do I will, and more I will
Than for myself I dare. Let that suffice you.

Iago. Is my lord angry?

Emilia.   He went hence but now,
And certainly in strange unquietness.

Iago. Can he be angry? I have seen the cannon
When it hath blown his ranks into the air
And, like the devil, from his very arm
Puff 'd his own brother—and can he be angry?
Something of moment then. I will go meet him:
There's matter in't indeed if he be angry.

Desdemona. I prithee, do so.

              Exit Iago.

      Something sure of state.
Either from Venice or some unhatch'd practice
Made demonstrable here in Cyprus to him,
Hath puddled his clear spirit, and in such cases
Men's natures wrangle with inferior things,
Though great ones are their object. 'Tis even so,
For let our finger ache, and it indues
Our other healthful members even to that sense
Of pain. Nay, we must think men are not gods
Nor of them look for such observancy
As fits the bridal. Beshrew me much, Emilia,
I was, unhandsome warrior as I am,

Arraigning his unkindness with my soul,
But now I find I had suborn'd the witness,
And he's indicted falsely.

Emilia. Pray heaven it be state matters, as you think,
And no conception nor no jealous toy
Concerning you.

Desdemona. Alas the day, I never gave him cause!

Emilia. But jealous souls will not be answer'd so;
They are not ever jealous for the cause,
But jealous for they are jealous. 'Tis a monster
Begot upon itself, born on itself.

Desdemona. Heaven keep that monster from Othello's mind!

Emilia. Lady, amen.

Desdemona. I will go seek him. Cassio, walk hereabout.
If I do find him fit, I'll move your suit,
And seek to effect it to my uttermost.

Cassio. I humbly thank your ladyship.

Exeunt Desdemona *and* Emilia.

Enter Bianca

Bianca. Save you, friend Cassio!

Cassio.   What make you from home?
How is it with you, my most fair Bianca?
I' faith, sweet love, I was coming to your house.

Bianca. And I was going to your lodging, Cassio.
What, keep a week away? Seven days and nights?
Eight score eight hours? And lovers' absent hours,
More tedious than the dial eight score times?
O weary reckoning!

Cassio.   Pardon me, Bianca,
I have this while with leaden thoughts been press'd,

But I shall in a more continuate time
Strike off this score of absence. Sweet Bianca,

> *Giving her* Desdemona's *handkerchief.*

Take me this work out.

Bianca.   O Cassio, whence came this?
This is some token from a newer friend!
To the felt absence now I feel a cause:
Is't come to this? Well, well.

Cassio.   Go to, woman!
Throw your vile guesses in the devil's teeth,
From whence you have them. You are jealous now
That this is from some mistress, some remembrance:
No, by my faith, Bianca.

Bianca.   Why, whose is it?

Cassio. I know not, sweet, I found it in my chamber.
I like the work well: ere it be demanded—
As like enough it will—I'd have it copied.
Take it, and do't, and leave me for this time.

Bianca. Leave you! Wherefore?

Cassio. I do attend here on the general
And think it no addition, nor my wish,
To have him see me woman'd.

Bianca.   Why, I pray you?

Cassio. Not that I love you not.

Bianca.   But that you do not love me.
I pray you, bring me on the way a little,
And say if I shall see you soon at night.

Cassio. 'Tis but a little way that I can bring you,
For I attend here. But I'll see you soon.

Bianca. 'Tis very good; I must be circumstanced.

> *Exeunt.*

act 4

scene 1. [*Cyprus. Before the castle*]

Enter Othello *and* Iago

Iago. Will you think so?

Othello.   Think so, Iago!

Iago.   What,
 To kiss in private?

Othello.   An unauthorized kiss.

Iago. Or to be naked with her friend in bed
 An hour or more, not meaning any harm?

Othello. Naked in bed, Iago, and not mean harm!
 It is hypocrisy against the devil:
 They that mean virtuously and yet do so,
 The devil their virtue tempts and they tempt heaven.

Iago. So they do nothing, 'tis a venial slip:
 But if I give my wife a handkerchief—

Othello. What then?

Iago. Why, then 'tis hers, my lord, and being hers
 She may, I think, bestow't on any man.

Othello. She is protectress of her honour too:
   May she give that?

Iago. Her honour is an essence that's not seen;
   They have it very oft that have it not.
   But for the handkerchief—

Othello. By heaven, I would most gladly have forgot it!
   Thou said'st—O, it comes o'er my memory
   As doth the raven o'er the infectious house,
   Boding to all—he had my handkerchief.

Iago. Ay, what of that?

Othello.   That's not so good now.

Iago. What If I had said I had seen him do you wrong?
   Or heard him say—as knaves be such abroad
   Who, having by their own importunate suit
   Or voluntary dotage of some mistress
   Convinced or supplied them, cannot choose
   But they must blab—

Othello.   Hath he said anything?

Iago. He hath, my lord, but be you well assured
   No more than he'll unswear.

Othello.   What hath he said?

Iago. Faith, that he did—I know not what he did.

Othello. What? What?

Iago. Lie—

Othello.   With her?

Iago.   With her, on her, what you will.

Othello. Lie with her! Lie on her!—We 'say lie on her, when
   they belie her.—Lie with her! 'Zounds, that's fulsome!
   Handkerchief—confessions—handkerchief!—To confess, and

be hanged for his labour. First to be hanged, and then to confess. I tremble at it. Nature would not invest herself in such shadowing passion without some instruction. It is not words that shakes me thus. Pish! Noses, ears and lips. Is't possible?—Confess?—Handkerchief?—O devil!

Falls in a trance.

Iago.　　Work on,
My medicine, work! Thus credulous fools are caught,
And many worthy and chaste dames even thus,
All guiltless, meet reproach. What, ho! My lord!
My lord, I say! Othello!

Enter Cassio
How now, Cassio!

Cassio. What's the matter?

Iago. My lord is fall'n into an epilepsy.
This is his second fit; he had one yesterday.

Cassio. Rub him about the temples.

Iago.　　　　　　　　　No, forbear.
The lethargy must have his quiet course;
If not, he foams at mouth, and by and by
Breaks out to savage madness. Look, he stirs.
Do you withdraw yourself a little while,
He will recover straight. When he is gone,
I would on great occasion speak with you.

Exit Cassio.
How is it, general? Have you not hurt your head?

Othello. Dost thou mock me?

Iago.　　　　　　　I mock you! No, by heaven.
Would you would bear your fortune like a man!

Othello. A horned man's a monster and a beast.

Iago. There's many a beast then in a populous city,
    And many a civil monster.

Othello. Did he confess it?

Iago.   Good sir, be a man,
    Think every bearded fellow that's but yoked
    May draw with you. There's millions now alive
    That nightly lie in those unproper beds
    Which they dare swear peculiar: your case is better.
    O, 'tis the spite of hell, the fiend's arch-mock,
    To lip a wanton in a secure couch,
    And to suppose her chaste! No, let me know,
    And knowing what I am, I know what she shall be.

Othello. O, thou art wise, 'tis certain.

Iago.   Stand you awhile apart,
    Confine yourself but in a patient list.
    Whilst you were here o'erwhelmed with your grief—
    A passion most unsuiting such a man—
    Cassio came hither. I shifted him away
    And laid good 'scuse upon your ecstasy,
    Bade him anon return and here speak with me,
    The which he promised. Do but encave yourself,
    And mark the fleers, the gibes and notable scorns,
    That dwell in every region of his face,
    For I will make him tell the tale anew,
    Where, how, how oft, how long ago, and when
    He hath and is again to cope your wife.
    I say, but mark his gesture. Marry, patience,
    Or I shall say you are all in all in spleen,
    And nothing of a man.

Othello.   Dost thou hear, Iago?
    I will be found most cunning in my patience
    But—dost thou hear?—most bloody.

Iago.   That's not amiss;
But yet keep time in all. Will you withdraw?

                                        Othello *retires.*

Now will I question Cassio of Bianca,
A housewife that by selling her desires
Buys herself bread and clothes: it is a creature
That dotes on Cassio, as 'tis the strumpet's plague
To beguile many and be beguiled by one.
He, when he hears of her, cannot refrain
From the excess of laughter. Here he comes.

                    Re-enter Cassio

As he shall smile, Othello shall go mad.
And his unbookish jealousy must construe
Poor Cassio's smiles, gestures and light behaviour
Quite in the wrong. How do you now, lieutenant?

Cassio. The worser that you give me the addition
Whose want even kills me.

Iago. Ply Desdemona well, and you are sure on't.
Now, if this suit lay in Bianca's power,
How quickly should you speed!

Cassio.   Alas, poor caitiff!

Othello. Look, how he laughs already!

Iago. I never knew a woman love man so.

Cassio. Alas, poor rogue! I think i' faith she loves me.

Othello. Now he denies it faintly and laughs it out.

Iago. Do you hear, Cassio?

Othello.   Now he importunes him
To tell it o'er: go to, well said, well said.

Iago. She gives it out that you shall marry her:
Do you intend it?

Cassio. Ha, ha, ha!

Othello. Do you triumph, Roman? Do you triumph?

Cassio. I marry her! What, a customer! I prithee, bear some charity to my wit; do not think it so unwholesome. Ha, ha, ha!

Othello. So, so, so, so: they laugh that win.

Iago. Faith, the cry goes that you shall marry her.

Cassio. Prithee say true.

Iago. I am a very villain else.

Othello. Have you scored me? Well.

Cassio. This is the monkey's own giving out. She is persuaded I will marry her, out of her own love and flattery, not out of my promise.

Othello. Iago beckons me; now he begins the story.

Cassio. She was here even now, she haunts me in every place. I was the other day talking on the sea-bank with certain Venetians, and thither comes the bauble and, by this hand, she falls me thus about my neck—

Othello. Crying 'O dear Cassio!' as it were: his gesture imports it.

Cassio. So hangs and lolls and weeps upon me, so hales and pulls me: ha, ha, ha!

Othello. Now he tells how she plucked him to my chamber. O, I see that nose of yours, but not that dog I shall throw it to.

Cassio. Well, I must leave her company.

Iago. Before me! Look where she comes.

Cassio. 'Tis such another fitchew! Marry, a perfumed one.

Enter Bianca

What do you mean by this haunting of me?

Bianca. Let the devil and his dam haunt you! What did you mean by that same handkerchief you gave me even now? I was a fine fool to take it. I must take out the work? A likely piece of work, that you should find it in your chamber and not know who left it there! This is some minx's token, and I must take out the work? There, give it your hobby-horse: wheresoever you had it, I'll take out no work on't.

Cassio. How now, my sweet Bianca! How now, how now!

Othello. By heaven, that should be my handkerchief!

Bianca. If you'll come to supper tonight, you may; if you will not, come when you are next prepared for.

Exit.

Iago. After her, after her.

Cassio. Faith, I must, she'll rail i' the streets else.

Iago. Will you sup there?

Cassio. Faith, I intend so.

Iago. Well, I may chance to see you, for I would very fain speak with you.

Cassio. Prithee come, will you?

Iago. Go to, say no more.

Exit Cassio.

Othello. [*Advancing*] How shall I murder him, Iago?

Iago. Did you perceive how he laughed at his vice?

Othello. O Iago!

Iago. And did you see the handkerchief?

Othello. Was that mine?

Iago. Yours, by this hand: and to see how he prizes the foolish woman your wife! She gave it him, and he hath given it his whore.

Othello. I would have him nine years a-killing. A fine woman, a fair woman, a sweet woman!

Iago. Nay, you must forget that.

Othello. Ay, let her rot and perish and be damned tonight, for she shall not live. No, my heart is turned to stone; I strike it, and it hurts my hand. O, the world hath not a sweeter creature: she might lie by an emperor's side, and command him tasks.

Iago. Nay, that's not your way.

Othello. Hang her! I do but say what she is: so delicate with her needle, an admirable musician. O, she will sing the savageness out of a bear! Of so high and plenteous wit and invention:—

Iago. She's the worse for all this.

Othello. O, a thousand thousand times: and then of so gentle a condition!

Iago. Ay, too gentle.

Othello. Nay, that's certain, but yet the pity of it, Iago!
O Iago, the pity of it, Iago!

Iago. If you are so fond over her iniquity, give her patent to offend, for if it touch not you, it comes near nobody.

Othello. I will chop her into messes! Cuckold me!

Iago. O, 'tis foul in her.

Othello. With mine officer!

Iago. That's fouler.

Othello. Get me some poison, Iago, this night. I'll not expostulate with her, lest her body and beauty unprovide my mind again. This night, Iago.

Iago. Do it not with poison. Strangle her in her bed, even the bed she hath contaminated.

Othello. Good, good. The justice of it pleases: very good.

Iago. And for Cassio, let me be his undertaker. You shall hear more by midnight.

Othello. Excellent good.

A trumpet within.

What trumpet is that same?

Iago. Something from Venice, sure. 'Tis Lodovico Come from
the duke, and see, your wife is with him.

Enter Lodovico, Desdemona, *and* Attendants

Lodovico. God save you, worthy general!

Othello.   With all my heart, sir.

Lodovico. The duke and senators of Venice greet you.

Gives him a letter.

Othello. I kiss the instrument of their pleasures.

Opens the letter and reads.

Desdemona. And what's the news, good cousin Lodovico?

Iago. I am very glad to see you, signior.
    Welcome to Cyprus.

Lodovico. I thank you. How does Lieutenant Cassio?

Iago. Lives, sir.

Desdemona. Cousin, there's fall'n between him and my lord
    An unkind breach, but you shall make all well.

Othello. Are you sure of that?

Desdemona. My lord?

Othello. [*Reads*] *This fail you not to do, as you will—*

Lodovico. He did not call, he's busy in the paper.
    Is there division 'twixt my lord and Cassio?

Desdemona. A most unhappy one: I would do much
    T' atone them, for the love I bear to Cassio.

Othello. Fire and brimstone!

Desdemona. My lord?

Othello. Are you wise?

Desdemona. What, is he angry?

Lodovico.   May be the letter moved him,
    For, as I think, they do command him home,
    Deputing Cassio in his government.

Desdemona. By my troth, I am glad on't.

Othello.   Indeed!

Desdemona.   My lord?

Othello. I am glad to see you mad.

Desdemona.   Why, sweet Othello?

Othello. Devil!

                                    Striking her.

Desdemona. I have not deserved this.

Lodovico. My lord, this would not be believed in Venice,
    Though I should swear I saw't. 'Tis very much.
    Make her amends, she weeps.

Othello.   O devil, devil!
    If that the earth could teem with woman's tears,
    Each drop she falls would prove a crocodile.
    Out of my sight!

Desdemona.   I will not stay to offend you.

                                            Going.

Lodovico. Truly, an obedient lady.
    I do beseech your lordship, call her back.

Othello. Mistress!

Desdemona. My lord?

Othello. What would you with her, sir?

Lodovico.   Who, I, my lord?

Othello. Ay, you did wish that I would make her turn.
    Sir, she can turn and turn, and yet go on,

And turn again; and she can weep, sir, weep.
And she's obedient, as you say, obedient,
Very obedient.
[*To Desdemona*] Proceed you in your tears.
Concerning this, sir—O well-painted passion!—
I am commanded home. Get you away;
I'll send for you anon. Sir, I obey the mandate
And will return to Venice. Hence, avaunt!

                                        Exit Desdemona.

Cassio shall have my place. And, sir, tonight
I do entreat that we may sup together.
You are welcome, sir, to Cyprus. Goats and monkeys!

                                        Exit.

Lodovico. Is this the noble Moor whom our full senate
    Call all in all sufficient? This the nature
    Whom passion could not shake? Whose solid virtue
    The shot of accident nor dart of chance
    Could neither graze nor pierce?

Iago.   He is much changed.

Lodovico. Are his wits safe? Is he not light of brain?

Iago. He's that he is: I may not breathe my censure
    What he might be: if what he might he is not,
    I would to heaven he were!

Lodovico.   What, strike his wife!

Iago. Faith, that was not so well, yet would I knew
    That stroke would prove the worst!

Lodovico.   Is it his use?
    Or did the letters work upon his blood,
    And new create this fault?

Iago.   Alas, alas!
    It is not honesty in me to speak
    What I have seen and known. You shall observe him,

And his own courses will denote him so
That I may save my speech. Do but go after
And mark how he continues.

Lodovico. I am sorry that I am deceived in him.

Exeunt.

scene 2. [*A room in the castle*]

Enter Othello *and* Emilia

Othello. You have seen nothing, then?

Emilia. Nor ever heard, nor ever did suspect.

Othello. Yes, you have seen Cassio and she together.

Emilia. But then I saw no harm, and then I heard
Each syllable that breath made up between them.

Othello. What, did they never whisper?

Emilia.   Never, my lord.

Othello. Nor send you out o' th' way?

Emilia. Never.

Othello. To fetch her fan, her gloves, her mask, nor nothing?

Emilia. Never, my lord.

Othello. That's strange.

Emilia. I durst, my lord, to wager she is honest,
Lay down my soul at stake: if you think other,
Remove your thought. It doth abuse your bosom.
If any wretch have put this in your head,
Let heaven requite it with the serpent's curse!
For if she be not honest, chaste and true
There's no man happy; the purest of their wives
Is foul as slander.

Othello.　　　　　　Bid her come hither: go.

　　　　　　　　　　　　　　　　Exit Emilia.

　　She says enough, yet she's a simple bawd

　　That cannot say as much. This is a subtle whore,

　　A closet lock and key of villanous secrets.

　　And yet she'll kneel and pray; I have seen her do't.

　　　　　　　Enter Desdemona *with* Emilia

Desdemona. My lord, what is your will?

Othello.　　　　　　　　　　Pray, chuck, come hither.

Desdemona. What is your pleasure?

Othello.　　　　　　　　Let me see your eyes;

　　Look in my face.

Desdemona.　　　　What horrible fancy's this?

Othello. [*To Emilia*] Some of your function, mistress,

　　Leave procreants alone and shut the door;

　　Cough, or cry hem, if anybody come.

　　Your mystery, your mystery: nay, dispatch.

　　　　　　　　　　　　　　　　Exit Emilia.

Desdemona. Upon my knees, what doth your speech import?

　　I understand a fury in your words,

　　But not the words.

Othello. Why, what art thou?

Desdemona. Your wife, my lord, your true and loyal wife.

Othello. Come, swear it, damn thyself,

　　Lest, being like one of heaven, the devils themselves

　　Should fear to seize thee: therefore be double-damn'd,

　　Swear thou art honest.

Desdemona.　　　　　　Heaven doth truly know it.

Othello. Heaven truly knows that thou art false as hell.

Desdemona. To whom, my lord? With whom? How am I false?

Othello. O Desdemona! Away, away, away!

Desdemona. Alas the heavy day! Why do you weep?
  Am I the motive of these tears, my lord?
  If haply you my father do suspect
  An instrument of this your calling back,
  Lay not your blame on me: if you have lost him,
  Why, I have lost him too.

Othello.   Had it pleased heaven
  To try me with affliction, had they rain'd
  All kinds of sores and shames on my bare head,
  Steep'd me in poverty to the very lips,
  Given to captivity me and my utmost hopes,
  I should have found in some place of my soul
  A drop of patience. But, alas, to make me
  A fixed figure for the time of scorn
  To point his slow and moving finger at!
  Yet could I bear that too, well, very well:
  But there, where I have garner'd up my heart,
  Where either I must live or bear no life,
  The fountain from the which my current runs
  Or else dries up—to be discarded thence!
  Or keep it as a cistern for foul toads
  To knot and gender in! Turn thy complexion there,
  Patience, thou young and rose-lipp'd cherubin,
  Ay, there look, grim as hell!

Desdemona. I hope my noble lord esteems me honest.

Othello. O, ay, as summer flies are in the shambles,
  That quicken even with blowing. O thou weed,
  Who art so lovely fair and smell'st so sweet
  That the sense aches at thee, would thou hadst ne'er been
  born!

Desdemona. Alas, what ignorant sin have I committed?

Othello. Was this fair paper, this most goodly book
Made to write 'whore' upon? What committed!
Committed? O thou public commoner!
I should make very forges of my cheeks,
That would to cinders burn up modesty,
Did I but speak thy deeds. What committed!
Heaven stops the nose at it, and the moon winks,
The bawdy wind that kisses all it meets
Is hush'd within the hollow mine of earth,
And will not hear it. What committed!
Impudent strumpet!

Desdemona.　　　　　By heaven, you do me wrong.

Othello. Are not you a strumpet?

Desdemona.　　　　　No, as I am a Christian.
If to preserve this vessel for my lord
From any other foul unlawful touch
Be not to be a strumpet, I am none.

Othello. What, not a whore?

Desdemona.　　　　　No, as I shall be saved.

Othello. Is't possible?

Desdemona. O, heaven forgive us!

Othello.　　　　　I cry you mercy then:
I took you for that cunning whore of Venice
That married with Othello. [*Raising his voice*] You, mistress,
That have the office opposite to Saint Peter
And keep the gate of hell!
　　　　　Re-enter Emilia
　　　　　You, you, ay, you!
We have done our course, there's money for your pains:
I pray you, turn the key and keep our counsel.

　　　　　　　　　　　　　　　　Exit.

Emilia. Alas, what does this gentleman conceive?
   How do you, madam? How do you, my good lady?

Desdemona. Faith, half asleep.

Emilia. Good madam, what's the matter with my lord?

Desdemona. With who?

Emilia. Why, with my lord, madam.

Desdemona. Who is thy lord?

Emilia.   He that is yours, sweet lady.

Desdemona. I have none. Do not talk to me, Emilia;
   I cannot weep, nor answer have I none
   But what should go by water. Prithee, tonight
   Lay on my bed my wedding sheets: remember,
   And call thy husband hither.

Emilia.   Here's a change indeed!

                                                Exit.

Desdemona. 'Tis meet I should be used so, very meet.
   How have I been behaved, that he might stick
   The small'st opinion on my greatest misuse?
                  Re-enter Emilia *with* Iago

Iago. What is your pleasure, madam? How is't with you?

Desdemona. I cannot tell. Those that do teach young babes
   Do it with gentle means and easy tasks.
   He might have chid me so, for in good faith
   I am a child to chiding.

Iago.   What's the matter, lady?

Emilia. Alas, Iago, my lord hath so bewhored her,
   Thrown such despite and heavy terms upon her
   As true hearts cannot bear.

Desdemona. Am I that name, Iago?

Iago.   What name, fair lady?

Desdemona. Such as she says my lord did say I was.

Emilia. He call'd her whore: a beggar in his drink
   Could not have laid such terms upon his callet.

Iago. Why did he so?

Desdemona. I do not know; I am sure I am none such.

Iago. Do not weep, do not weep. Alas the day!

Emilia. Hath she forsook so many noble matches,
   Her father and her country and her friends,
   To be call'd whore? Would it not make one weep?

Desdemona. It is my wretched fortune.

Iago.   Beshrew him for't!
   How comes this trick upon him?

Desdemona.   Nay, heaven doth know.

Emilia. I will be hang'd if some eternal villain,
   Some busy and insinuating rogue,
   Some cogging, cozening slave, to get some office,
   Have not devised this slander; I'll be hang'd else.

Iago. Fie, there is no such man, it is impossible.

Desdemona. If any such there be, heaven pardon him!

Emilia. A halter pardon him, and hell gnaw his bones!
   Why should he call her whore? Who keeps her company?
   What place, what time, what form, what likelihood?
   The Moor's abused by some most villanous knave,
   Some base notorious knave, some scurvy fellow.
   O heaven, that such companions thou 'dst unfold,
   And put in every honest hand a whip
   To lash the rascals naked through the world
   Even from the east to the west!

Iago.   Speak within doors.

Emilia. O, fie upon them! Some such squire he was
    That turn'd your wit the seamy side without,
    And made you to suspect me with the Moor.

Iago. You are a fool, go to.

Desdemona.   O good Iago,
    What shall I do to win my lord again?
    Good friend, go to him, for, by this light of heaven,
    I know not how I lost him. Here I kneel:
    If e'er my will did trespass 'gainst his love
    Either in discourse of thought or actual deed,
    Or that mine eyes, mine ears, or any sense
    Delighted them in any other form,
    Or that I do not yet, and ever did,
    And ever will-though he do shake me off
    To beggarly divorcement-love him dearly,
    Comfort forswear me! Unkindness may do much,
    And his unkindness may defeat my life
    But never taint my love. I cannot say 'whore':
    It doth abhor me now I speak the word;
    To do the act that might the addition earn
    Not the world's mass of vanity could make me.

Iago. I pray you, be content, 'tis but his humour:
    The business of the state does him offence
    And he does chide with you.

Desdemona. If 'twere no other—

Iago.   'Tis but so, I warrant.
                      Trumpets within.
    Hark, how these instruments summon to supper!
    The messengers of Venice stay the meat:
    Go in, and weep not; all things shall be well.
                  Exeunt Desdemona *and* Emilia.

Enter Roderigo

How now, Roderigo!

Roderigo. I do not find that thou dealest justly with me.

Iago. What in the contrary?

Roderigo. Every day thou doffest me with some device, Iago, and rather, as it seems to me now, keepest from me all conveniency than suppliest me with the least advantage of hope. I will indeed no longer endure it, nor am I yet persuaded to put up in peace what already I have foolishly suffered.

Iago. Will you hear me, Roderigo?

Roderigo. Faith, I have heard too much, for your words and performances are no kin together.

Iago. You charge me most unjustly.

Roderigo. With nought but truth. I have wasted myself out of my means. The jewels you have had from me to deliver to Desdemona would half have corrupted a votarist. You have told me she hath received them and returned me expectations and comforts of sudden respect and acquaintance, but I find none.

Iago. Well, go to; very well.

Roderigo. 'Very well'! 'Go to'! I cannot go to, man, nor 'tis not very well. By this hand, I say 'tis very scurvy, and begin to find myself fopped in it.

Iago. Very well.

Roderigo. I tell you 'tis not very well! I will make myself known to Desdemona: if she will return me my jewels, I will give over my suit and repent my unlawful solicitation; if not, assure yourself I will seek satisfaction of you.

Iago. You have said now.

Roderigo. Ay, and said nothing but what I protest intendment of doing.

Iago. Why, now I see there's mettle in thee, and even from this instant do build on thee a better opinion than ever before. Give me thy hand, Roderigo. Thou hast taken against me a most just exception, but yet I protest I have dealt most directly in thy affair.

Roderigo. It hath not appeared.

Iago. I grant indeed it hath not appeared, and your suspicion is not without wit and judgement. But, Roderigo, if thou hast that in thee indeed, which I have greater reason to believe now than ever—I mean purpose, courage and valour—this night show it. If thou the next night following enjoy not Desdemona, take me from this world with treachery and devise engines for my life.

Roderigo. Well, what is it? Is it within reason and compass?

Iago. Sir, there is especial commission come from Venice to depute Cassio in Othello's place.

Roderigo. Is that true? Why then Othello and Desdemona return again to Venice.

Iago. O no, he goes into Mauritania and takes away with him the fair Desdemona, unless his abode be lingered here by some accident, wherein none can be so determinate as the removing of Cassio.

Roderigo. How do you mean, removing of him?

Iago. Why, by making him uncapable of Othello's place: knocking out his brains.

Roderigo. And that you would have me to do?

Iago. Ay, if you dare do yourself a profit and a right. He sups tonight with a harlotry, and thither will I go to him. He knows not yet of his honourable fortune. If you will watch his going thence, which I will fashion to fall out between twelve and one, you may take him at your pleasure. I will be near to second your attempt, and he shall fall between us. Come, stand not amazed at it, but go along with me; I will show you such a necessity in his death that you shall think yourself bound to put it on him. It is now high supper-time, and the night grows to waste: about it.

Roderigo. I will hear further reason for this.

Iago. And you shall be satisfied.

Exeunt.

scene 3.   [*Another room in the castle*]

Enter Othello, Lodovico, Desdemona, Emilia, *and* Attendants

Lodovico. I do beseech you, sir, trouble yourself no further.

Othello. O, pardon me, 'twill do me good to walk.

Lodovico. Madam, good night; I humbly thank your ladyship.

Desdemona. Your honour is most welcome.

Othello.   Will you walk, sir?
   O,—Desdemona,—

Desdemona. My lord?

Othello. Get you to bed on th' instant, I will be returned forthwith. Dismiss your attendant there: look it be done.

Desdemona. I will, my lord.

Exeunt Othello, Lodovico, *and* Attendants.

Emilia. How goes it now? He looks gentler than he did.

Desdemona. He says he will return incontinent:
    He hath commanded me to go to bed
    And bade me to dismiss you.

Emilia.   Dismiss me?

Desdemona. It was his bidding; therefore, good Emilia,
    Give me my nightly wearing, and adieu.
    We must not now displease him.

Emilia. I would you had never seen him!

Desdemona. So would not I: my love doth so approve him
    That even his stubbornness, his checks, his frowns—
    Prithee unpin me—have grace and favour in them.

Emilia. I have laid those sheets you bade me on the bed.

Desdemona. All's one. Good faith, how foolish are our minds!
    If I do die before thee, prithee shroud me
    In one of those same sheets.

Emilia.   Come, come, you talk.

Desdemona. My mother had a maid call'd Barbary:
    She was in love, and he she loved proved mad
    And did forsake her. She had a song of 'willow';
    An old thing 'twas, but it express'd her fortune
    And she died singing it. That song tonight
    Will not go from my mind. I have much to do
    But to go hang my head all at one side
    And sing it like poor Barbary. Prithee dispatch.

Emilia. Shall I go fetch your night-gown?

Desdemona.   No, unpin me here.
    This Lodovico is a proper man.

Emilia. A very handsome man.

Desdemona. He speaks well.

Emilia. I know a lady in Venice would have walked barefoot to
    Palestine for a touch of his nether lip.

Desdemona. [*Singing*]
>   The poor soul sat sighing by a sycamore tree,
>   Sing all a green willow;
>   Her hand on her bosom, her head on her knee,
>   Sing willow, willow, willow.
>   The fresh streams ran by her and murmur'd her moans,
>   Sing willow, willow, willow;
>   Her salt tears fell from her, and soften'd the stones—

Lay by these:—

[*Singing*]
>   Sing willow, willow, willow.

Prithee hie thee; he'll come anon:—

[*Singing*]
>   Sing all a green willow must be my garland.
>   Let nobody blame him, his scorn I approve—

Nay, that's not next. Hark! Who is't that knocks?

Emilia. It's the wind.

Desdemona. [*Singing*]
>   I call'd my love false love, but what said he then?
>   Sing willow, willow, willow;
>   If I court moe women, you'll couch with moe men.

So get thee gone; good night. Mine eyes do itch.
Doth that bode weeping?

Emilia.   'Tis neither here nor there.

Desdemona. I have heard it said so. O, these men, these men!
Dost thou in conscience think—tell me, Emilia—
That there be women do abuse their husbands
In such gross kind?

Emilia.   There be some such, no question.

Desdemona. Wouldst thou do such a deed for all the world?

Emilia. Why, would not you?

Desdemona.   No, by this heavenly light!

Emilia. Nor I neither by this heavenly light; I might do't as well
i' the dark.

Desdemona. Wouldst thou do such a deed for all the world?

Emilia. The world's a huge thing: it is a great price
For a small vice.

Desdemona. Good troth, I think thou wouldst not.

Emilia. By my troth, I think I should, and undo 't when I had
done. Marry, I would not do such a thing for a joint-ring,
nor for measures of lawn, nor for gowns, petticoats, nor caps,
nor any petty exhibition, but for the whole world—why,
who would not make her husband a cuckold to make him a
monarch? I should venture purgatory for 't.

Desdemona. Beshrew me, if I would do such a wrong
For the whole world.

Emilia. Why, the wrong is but a wrong i' th' world; and having
the world for your labour, 'tis a wrong in your own world,
and you might quickly make it right.

Desdemona. I do not think there is any such woman.

Emilia. Yes, a dozen, and as many to the vantage as would store
the world they played for.
But I do think it is their husbands' faults
If wives do fall. Say that they slack their duties
And pour our treasures into foreign laps,
Or else break out in peevish jealousies,
Throwing restraint upon us, or say they strike us,
Or scant our former having in despite,
Why, we have galls, and though we have some grace
Yet have we some revenge. Let husbands know
Their wives have sense like them: they see and smell
And have their palates both for sweet and sour,

As husbands have. What is it that they do
When they change us for others? Is it sport?
I think it is. And doth affection breed it?
I think it doth. Is't frailty that thus errs?
It is so too. And have not we affections,
Desires for sport, and frailty, as men have?
Then let them use us well: else let them know,
The ills we do, their ills instruct us so.

Desdemona. Good night, good night. God me such uses send,
Not to pick bad from bad, but by bad mend!

Exeunt.

act 5

scene 1. [*Cyprus. A street*]

Enter Iago *and* Roderigo

Iago. Here, stand behind this bulk, straight will he come.
　Wear thy good rapier bare, and put it home:
　Quick, quick, fear nothing, I'll be at thy elbow.
　It makes us or it mars us, think on that
　And fix most firm thy resolution.

Roderigo. Be near at hand, I may miscarry in't.

Iago. Here, at thy hand: be bold, and take thy stand.

Retires.

Roderigo. I have no great devotion to the deed
　And yet he hath given me satisfying reasons:
　'Tis but a man gone. Forth, my sword: he dies.

Iago. I have rubb'd this young quat almost to the sense,
　And he grows angry. Now, whether he kill Cassio,
　Or Cassio him, or each do kill the other,
　Every way makes my gain. Live Roderigo,
　He calls me to a restitution large
　Of gold and jewels that I bobb'd from him

As gifts to Desdemona:
It must not be. If Cassio do remain,
He hath a daily beauty in his life
That makes me ugly; and besides, the Moor
May unfold me to him—there stand I in much peril.
No, he must die. Be't so. I hear him coming.

Enter Cassio

Roderigo. I know his gait; 'tis he. Villain, thou diest!

Charges at Cassio.

Cassio. That thrust had been mine enemy indeed,
But that my coat is better than thou know'st:
I will make proof of thine.

Draws, and wounds Roderigo.

Roderigo. O, I am slain!

Iago *from behind wounds* Cassio *in the leg, and exits.*

Cassio. I am maim'd forever. Help, ho! Murder! Murder!

Falls.

Enter Othello

Othello. The voice of Cassio. Iago keeps his word.

Roderigo. O, villain that I am!

Othello. It is even so.

Cassio. O, help, ho! Light! A surgeon!

Othello. 'Tis he. O brave Iago, honest and just,
That hast such noble sense of thy friend's wrong!
Thou teachest me. Minion, your dear lies dead,
And your unblest fate hies: strumpet, I come!
Forth of my heart those charms, thine eyes, are blotted.
Thy bed lust-stain'd shall with lust's blood be spotted.

Exit.

Enter Lodovico *and* Gratiano

Cassio. What, ho! No watch, no passage? Murder!
Murder!

Gratiano. 'Tis some mischance, the cry is very direful.

Cassio. O help!

Lodovico. Hark!

Roderigo. O wretched villain!

Lodovico. Two or three groan: it is a heavy night.
These may be counterfeits; let's think't unsafe
To come in to the cry without more help.

Roderigo. Nobody come? Then shall I bleed to death.

Lodovico. Hark!

            Re-enter Iago, *with a light*

Gratiano. Here's one comes in his shirt, with light and weapons.

Iago. Who's there? Whose noise is this that cries on murder?

Lodovico. We do not know.

Iago.   Did not you hear a cry?

Cassio. Here, here! For heaven's sake, help me!

Iago.   What's the matter?

Gratiano. This is Othello's ancient, as I take it.

Lodovico. The same indeed, a very valiant fellow.

Iago. What are you here that cry so grievously?

Cassio. Iago? O, I am spoil'd, undone by villains!
Give me some help.

Iago. O me, lieutenant! What villains have done this?

Cassio. I think that one of them is hereabout
And cannot make away.

Iago.   O treacherous villains!
What are you there? Come in and give some help.

                          To Lodovico *and* Gratiano.

Roderigo. O, help me here!

Cassio. That's one of them.

Iago.   O murderous slave! O villain!

                                                   Stabs Roderigo.

Roderigo. O damn'd Iago! O inhuman dog!

Iago. Kill men i' the dark! Where be these bloody thieves?
    How silent is this town! Ho, murder! Murder!
    What may you be? Are you of good or evil?

Lodovico. As you shall prove us, praise us.

Iago. Signior Lodovico?

Lodovico. He, sir.

Iago. I cry you mercy. Here's Cassio hurt by villains.

Gratiano. Cassio!

Iago. How is't, brother?

Cassio. My leg is cut in two.

Iago.   Marry, heaven forbid!
    Light, gentlemen, I'll bind it with my shirt.

                           Enter Bianca

Bianca. What is the matter, ho? Who is't that cried?

Iago. Who is't that cried?

Bianca. O my dear Cassio! My sweet Cassio! O Cassio,
    Cassio, Cassio!

Iago. O notable strumpet! Cassio, may you suspect
    Who they should be that have thus mangled you?

Cassio. No.

Gratiano. I am sorry to find you thus; I have been to seek you.

Iago. Lend me a garter. So. O for a chair,
    To bear him easily hence!

Bianca. Alas, he faints! O Cassio, Cassio, Cassio!

Iago. Gentlemen all, I do suspect this trash
　　To be a party in this injury.
　　Patience awhile, good Cassio. Come, come,
　　Lend me a light. Know we this face or no?
　　Alas, my friend and my dear countryman
　　Roderigo? No—yes, sure—O heaven! Roderigo.

Gratiano. What, of Venice?

Iago. Even he, sir. Did you know him?

Gratiano. 　　　　　　　　　Know him! Ay.

Iago. Signior Gratiano? I cry you gentle pardon.
　　These bloody accidents must excuse my manners
　　That so neglected you.

Gratiano. 　　　　　　　I am glad to see you.

Iago. How do you, Cassio? O, a chair, a chair!

Gratiano. Roderigo!

Iago. He, he, 'tis he.

　　　　　　　　　　　　　　A chair is brought in.

　　O, that's well said, the chair.
　　Some good man bear him carefully from hence,
　　I'll fetch the general's surgeon.
　　[*To Bianca*] For you, mistress,
　　Save you your labour. He that lies slain here, Cassio,
　　Was my dear friend. What malice was between you?

Cassio. None in the world, nor do I know the man.

Iago. [*To Bianca*] What, look you pale? O, bear him out o' th' air.
　　　　　　　　　Cassio and Roderigo *are borne off.*
　　Stay you, good gentlemen. Look you pale, mistress?
　　Do you perceive the gastness of her eye?
　　Nay, if you stare, we shall hear more anon.

Behold her well, I pray you, look upon her:
Do you see, gentlemen? Nay, guiltiness will speak,
Though tongues were out of use.

Enter Emilia

Emilia. 'Las, what's the matter? What's the matter, husband?

Iago. Cassio hath here been set on in the dark
By Roderigo and fellows that are 'scaped:
He's almost slain, and Roderigo dead.

Emilia. Alas, good gentleman! Alas, good Cassio!

Iago. This is the fruit of whoring. Prithee, Emilia,
Go know of Cassio where he supp'd tonight.
What, do you shake at that?

Bianca. He supp'd at my house, but I therefore shake not.

Iago. O, did he so? I charge you, go with me.

Emilia. Fie, fie upon thee, strumpet!

Bianca. I am no strumpet, but of life as honest
As you that thus abuse me.

Emilia.   As I! Foh, fie upon thee!

Iago. Kind gentlemen, let's go see poor Cassio dress'd.
Come, mistress, you must tell's another tale.
Emilia, run you to the citadel,
And tell my lord and lady what hath happ'd.
Will you go on, I pray? [*Aside*] This is the night
That either makes me or fordoes me quite.

Exeunt.

scene 2. [*A bedchamber in the castle:*
Desdemona *in bed asleep; a light burning*]

Enter Othello

Othello. It is the cause, it is the cause, my soul.
  Let me not name it to you, you chaste stars!
  It is the cause. Yet I'll not shed her blood
  Nor scar that whiter skin of hers than snow
  And smooth as monumental alabaster.
  Yet she must die, else she'll betray more men.
  Put out the light, and then put out the light.
  If I quench thee, thou flaming minister,
  I can again thy former light restore
  Should I repent me. But once put out thy light,
  Thou cunning'st pattern of excelling nature,
  I know not where is that Promethean heat
  That can thy light relume. When I have pluck'd the rose,
  I cannot give it vital growth again,
  It must needs wither. I'll smell it on the tree.

                                        Kissing her.

  Ah, balmy breath, that dost almost persuade
  Justice to break her sword! Once more, once more:
  Be thus when thou art dead, and I will kill thee
  And love thee after. Once more, and this the last.
  So sweet was ne'er so fatal. I must weep,
  But they are cruel tears. This sorrow's heavenly,
  It strikes where it doth love. She wakes.

Desdemona. Who's there? Othello?

Othello.   Ay, Desdemona.

Desdemona. Will you come to bed, my lord?

Othello. Have you pray'd tonight, Desdemon?

Desdemona. Ay, my lord.

Othello. If you bethink yourself of any crime
Unreconciled as yet to heaven and grace,
Solicit for it straight.

Desdemona. Alas, my lord, what may you mean by that?

Othello. Well, do it, and be brief; I will walk by.
I would not kill thy unprepared spirit.
No, heaven forfend, I would not kill thy soul.

Desdemona. Talk you of killing?

Othello. Ay, I do.

Desdemona. Then heaven have mercy on me!

Othello. Amen, with all my heart.

Desdemona. If you say so, I hope you will not kill me.

Othello. Hum!

Desdemona. And yet I fear you, for you are fatal then
When your eyes roll so. Why I should fear I know not,
Since guiltiness I know not. But yet I feel I fear.

Othello. Think on thy sins.

Desdemona.   They are loves I bear to you.

Othello. Ay, and for that thou diest.

Desdemona. That death's unnatural that kills for loving.
Alas, why gnaw you so your nether lip?
Some bloody passion shakes your very frame.
These are portents, but yet I hope, I hope
They do not point on me.

Othello.   Peace, and be still.

Desdemona. I will so. What's the matter?

Othello. That handkerchief which I so loved and gave thee,
    Thou gavest to Cassio.

Desdemona.   No, by my life and soul!
    Send for the man and ask him.

Othello.   Sweet soul, take heed,
    Take heed of perjury. Thou art on thy death-bed.

Desdemona. I? But not yet to die.

Othello.   Yes, presently.
    Therefore confess thee freely of thy sin,
    For to deny each article with oath
    Cannot remove nor choke the strong conception
    That I do groan withal. Thou art to die.

Desdemona. Then Lord have mercy on me!

Othello.   I say amen.

Desdemona. And have you mercy too! I never did
    Offend you in my life, never loved Cassio
    But with such general warranty of heaven
    As I might love: I never gave him token.

Othello. By heaven, I saw my handkerchief in's hand!
    O perjured woman, thou dost stone my heart
    And makest me call what I intend to do
    A murder, which I thought a sacrifice!
    I saw the handkerchief.

Desdemona.   He found it then,
    I never gave it him. Send for him hither,
    Let him confess a truth.

Othello.   He hath confess'd.

Desdemona. What, my lord?

Othello. That he hath used thee.

Desdemona.   How? Unlawfully?

Othello. Ay.

Desdemona. He will not say so.

Othello.   No, his mouth is stopp'd.
  Honest Iago hath ta'en order for't.

Desdemona. O, my fear interprets! What, is he dead?

Othello. Had all his hairs been lives, my great revenge
  Had stomach for them all.

Desdemona. Alas, he is betray'd, and I undone!

Othello. Out, strumpet! Weep'st thou for him to my face?

Desdemona. O, banish me, my lord, but kill me not!

Othello. Down, strumpet!

Desdemona. Kill me tomorrow, let me live tonight!

Othello. Nay, if you strive—

Desdemona. But half an hour!

Othello.   Being done, there is no pause.

Desdemona. But while I say one prayer!

Othello.   It is too late.

                                        He stifles her.

Emilia. [*Within*] My lord, my lord! What, ho! My lord, my lord!

Othello. What noise is this? Not dead? Not yet quite dead?
  I that am cruel am yet merciful;
  I would not have thee linger in thy pain.
  So, so.

Emilia. [*Within*] What, ho! My lord, my lord!

Othello.   Who's there?

Emilia. [*Within*] O good my lord, I'd speak a word with you!

Othello. Yes: 'tis Emilia. By and by. She's dead.
  'Tis like she comes to speak of Cassio's death,

The noise was high. Ha, no more moving?
Still as the grave. Shall she come in? Were't good?
I think she stirs again. No. What's best to do?
If she come in, she'll sure speak to my wife.
My wife, my wife! What wife? I have no wife.
O insupportable! O heavy hour!
Methinks it should be now a huge eclipse
Of sun and moon, and that th' affrighted globe
Should yawn at alteration.

Emilia. [*Within*]   I do beseech you
That I may speak with you, O good my lord!

Othello. I had forgot thee: O come in, Emilia.
Soft, by and by. Let me the curtains draw.
Where art thou?

Unlocks the door.

Enter Emilia
What's the matter with thee now?

Emilia. O, my good lord, yonder's foul murders done!

Othello. What, now?

Emilia. But now, my lord.

Othello. It is the very error of the moon;
She comes more nearer earth than she was wont
And makes men mad.

Emilia. Cassio, my lord, hath kill'd a young Venetian
Call'd Roderigo.

Othello.   Roderigo kill'd!
And Cassio kill'd?

Emilia.   No, Cassio is not kill'd.

Othello. Not Cassio kill'd! Then murder's out of tune,
And sweet revenge grows harsh.

Desdemona. O, falsely, falsely murder'd!

Emilia. Alas, what cry is that?

Othello. That! What?

Emilia. Out and alas! That was my lady's voice.
    Help, help, ho! Help! O lady, speak again!
    Sweet Desdemona, O sweet mistress, speak!

Desdemona. A guiltless death I die.

Emilia. O, who hath done this deed?

Desdemona. Nobody; I myself. Farewell.
    Commend me to my kind lord: O, farewell!

                                                              Dies.

Othello. Why, how should she be murder'd?

Emilia. Alas, who knows?

Othello. You heard her say herself, it was not I.

Emilia. She said so: I must needs report the truth.

Othello. She's like a liar gone to burning hell:
    'Twas I that kill'd her.

Emilia. O, the more angel she,
    And you the blacker devil!

Othello. She turn'd to folly, and she was a whore.

Emilia. Thou dost belie her, and thou art a devil.

Othello. She was false as water.

Emilia. Thou art rash as fire, to say
    That she was false. O, she was heavenly true!

Othello. Cassio did top her, ask thy husband else.
    O, I were damn'd beneath all depth in hell,
    But that I did proceed upon just grounds
    To this extremity. Thy husband knew it all.

Emilia. My husband?

Othello. Thy husband.

Emilia. That she was false to wedlock?

Othello. Ay, with Cassio. Nay, had she been true,
   If heaven would make me such another world
   Of one entire and perfect chrysolite,
   I'd not have sold her for it.

Emilia. My husband?

Othello.   Ay, 'twas he that told me first.
   An honest man he is, and hates the slime
   That sticks on filthy deeds.

Emilia.   My husband!

Othello. What needs this iteration, woman? I say thy husband.

Emilia. O mistress, villany hath made mocks with love!
   My husband say she was false!

Othello.   He, woman;
   I say thy husband: dost understand the word?
   My friend, thy husband, honest, honest Iago.

Emilia. If he say so, may his pernicious soul
   Rot half a grain a day! He lies to th' heart:
   She was too fond of her most filthy bargain!

Othello. Ha!

Emilia. Do thy worst:
   This deed of thine is no more worthy heaven
   Than thou wast worthy her.

Othello.   Peace, you were best!

Emilia. Thou hast not half that power to do me harm
   As I have to be hurt. O gull! O dolt!
   As ignorant as dirt! thou hast done a deed—

                              He brandishes his sword.

I care not for thy sword, I'll make thee known
Though I lost twenty lives. Help, help, ho, help!
The Moor hath kill'd my mistress! Murder, murder!

Enter Montano, Gratiano, Iago, *and others*

Montano. What is the matter? How now, general!

Emilia. O, are you come, Iago? You have done well,
That men must lay their murders on your neck.

Gratiano. What is the matter?

Emilia. Disprove this villain, if thou be'st a man.
He says thou told'st him that his wife was false:
I know thou didst not, thou'rt not such a villain.
Speak, for my heart is full.

Iago. I told him what I thought, and told no more
Than what he found himself was apt and true.

Emilia. But did you ever tell him she was false?

Iago. I did.

Emilia. You told a lie, an odious, damned lie!
Upon my soul, a lie, a wicked lie!
She false with Cassio! Did you say with Cassio?

Iago. With Cassio, mistress. Go to, charm your tongue.

Emilia. I will not charm my tongue, I am bound to speak:
My mistress here lies murder'd in her bed—

All. O heavens forfend!

Emilia. And your reports have set the murder on.

Othello. Nay, stare not, masters: it is true indeed.

Gratiano. 'Tis a strange truth.

Montano. O monstrous act!

Emilia. Villany, villany, villany!
I think upon't, I think I smell't, O villany!

I thought so then: I'll kill myself for grief!
O villany, villany!

Iago. What, are you mad? I charge you, get you home.

Emilia. Good gentlemen, let me have leave to speak.
'Tis proper I obey him, but not now.
Perchance, Iago, I will ne'er go home.

Othello. O! O! O!

Falling on the bed.

Emilia.   Nay, lay thee down and roar,
For thou hast kill'd the sweetest innocent
That e'er did lift up eye.

Othello. [*Rising*]   O, she was foul!
I scarce did know you, uncle: there lies your niece
Whose breath indeed these hands have newly stopp'd:
I know this act shows horrible and grim.

Gratiano. Poor Desdemon! I am glad thy father's dead:
Thy match was mortal to him, and pure grief
Shore his old thread in twain. Did he live now,
This sight would make him do a desperate turn,
Yea, curse his better angel from his side
And fall to reprobation.

Othello. 'Tis pitiful; but yet Iago knows
That she with Cassio hath the act of shame
A thousand times committed. Cassio confess'd it,
And she did gratify his amorous works
With that recognizance and pledge of love
Which I first gave her. I saw it in his hand:
It was a handkerchief, an antique token
My father gave my mother.

Emilia. O God! O heavenly God!

Iago. 'Zounds, hold your peace!

Emilia.   'Twill out, 'twill out! I peace?
  No, I will speak as liberal as the north:
  Let heaven and men and devils, let them all,
  All, all cry shame against me, yet I'll speak.

Iago. Be wise, and get you home.

Emilia.   I will not.

                      Iago *tries to stab* Emilia.

Gratiano.   Fie!
  Your sword upon a woman?

Emilia. O thou dull Moor! That handkerchief thou speak'st of
  I found by fortune and did give my husband,
  For often with a solemn earnestness,
  More than indeed belong'd to such a trifle,
  He begg'd of me to steal it.

Iago.   Villanous whore!

Emilia. She give it Cassio! No, alas, I found it
  And I did give't my husband.

Iago.   Filth, thou liest!

Emilia. By heaven, I do not, I do not, gentlemen.
  O murderous coxcomb! What should such a fool
  Do with so good a wife?

Othello.   Are there no stones in heaven
  But what serve for the thunder? Precious villain!
     He runs at Iago. Iago, *from behind, stabs* Emilia, *and exit.*

Gratiano. The woman falls, sure, he hath kill'd his wife.

Emilia. Ay, ay. O, lay me by my mistress' side.

Gratiano. He's gone, but his wife's kill'd

Montano. 'Tis a notorious villain. Take you this weapon,
  Which I have here recover'd from the Moor.
  Come, guard the door without, let him not pass

But kill him rather. I'll after that same villain,
For 'tis a damned slave.

Exeunt all but Othello *and* Emilia.

Othello.   I am not valiant neither,
But every puny whipster gets my sword.
But why should honour outlive honesty?
Let it go all.

Emilia.   What did thy song bode, lady?
Hark, canst thou hear me? I will play the swan
And die in music.

[*Singing*]
Willow, willow, willow.

Moor, she was chaste, she loved thee, cruel Moor,
So come my soul to bliss, as I speak true.
So speaking as I think, I die, I die.

Dies.

Othello. I have another weapon in this chamber,
It is a sword of Spain, the ice-brook's temper:—
O, here it is. Uncle, I must come forth.

Gratiano. [*Within*] If thou attempt it, it will cost thee dear:
Thou hast no weapon, and perforce must suffer.

Othello. Look in upon me then, and speak with me,
Or, naked as I am, I will assault thee.

Re-enter Gratiano

Gratiano. What is the matter?

Othello.   Behold, I have a weapon,
A better never did itself sustain
Upon a soldier's thigh. I have seen the day
That with this little arm and this good sword
I have made my way through more impediments
Than twenty times your stop: but, O vain boast!

Who can control his fate? 'Tis not so now.
Be not afraid, though you do see me weapon'd;
Here is my journey's end, here is my butt
And very sea-mark of my utmost sail.
Do you go back dismay'd? 'Tis a lost fear:
Man but a rush against. Othello's breast
And he retires. Where should Othello go?
Now, how dost thou look now? O ill-starr'd wench,
Pale as thy smock. When we shall meet at compt,
This look of thine will hurl my soul from heaven
And fiends will snatch at it. Cold, cold, my girl!
Even like thy chastity. O cursed slave!
Whip me, ye devils,
From the possession of this heavenly sight!
Blow me about in winds, roast me in sulphur!
Wash me in steep-down gulfs of liquid fire!
O Desdemona! Desdemona, dead!
O, o, o.

> *Enter* Lodovico, Montano, Cassio *carried in a chair,*
> *and* Officers *with* Iago, *prisoner*

Lodovico. Where is this rash and most unfortunate man?

Othello. That's he that was Othello? Here I am.

Lodovico. Where is that viper? Bring the villain forth.

Othello. I look down towards his feet, but that's a fable.
If that thou be'st a devil, I cannot kill thee.

> *Wounds* Iago.

Lodovico. Wrench his sword from him.

Iago.   I bleed, sir, but not kill'd.

Othello. I am not sorry neither: I'd have thee live,
For, in my sense, 'tis happiness to die.

Lodovico. O thou Othello, that wert once so good,
  Fall'n in the practice of a damned slave,
  What shall be said to thee?

Othello.   Why, anything:
  An honourable murderer, if you will,
  For nought did I in hate, but all in honour.

Lodovico. This wretch hath part confess'd his villany:
  Did you and he consent in Cassio's death?

Othello. Ay.

Cassio. Dear general, I never gave you cause.

Othello. I do believe it, and I ask your pardon.
  Will you, I pray, demand that demi-devil
  Why he hath thus ensnared my soul and body?

Iago. Demand me nothing. What you know, you know.
  From this time forth I never will speak word.

Lodovico. What, not to pray?

Gratiano.   Torments will ope your lips.

Othello. Well, thou dost best.

Lodovico. Sir, you shall understand what hath befall'n,
  Which, as I think, you know not. Here is a letter
  Found in the pocket of the slain Roderigo,
  And here another: the one of them imports
  The death of Cassio to be undertook
  By Roderigo.

Othello. O villain!

Cassio.   Most heathenish and most gross!

Lodovico. Now here's another discontented paper
  Found in his pocket too, and this, it seems,
  Roderigo meant to have sent this damned villain,

But that, belike, Iago in the interim
Came in and satisfied him.

Othello.   O the pernicious caitiff!
How came you, Cassio, by that handkerchief
That was my wife's?

Cassio.   I found it in my chamber,
And he himself confess'd but even now
That there he dropp'd it for a special purpose
Which wrought to his desire.

Othello.   O fool, fool, fool!

Cassio. There is besides in Roderigo's letter
How he upbraids Iago, that he made him
Brave me upon the watch; whereon it came
That I was cast, and even but now he spake
After long seeming dead, Iago hurt him,
Iago set him on.

Lodovico. You must forsake this room and go with us.
Your power and your command is taken off,
And Cassio rules in Cyprus. For this slave,
If there be any cunning cruelty
That can torment him much and hold him long,
It shall be his. You shall close prisoner rest,
Till that the nature of your fault be known
To the Venetian state. Come, bring him away.

Othello. Soft you; a word or two before you go.
I have done the state some service, and they know't.
No more of that. I pray you, in your letters,
When you shall these unlucky deeds relate,
Speak of me as I am. Nothing extenuate,
Nor set down aught in malice. Then must you speak
Of one that loved not wisely but too well;
Of one not easily jealous, but, being wrought,

Perplex'd in the extreme; of one whose hand,
Like the base Indian, threw a pearl away
Richer than all his tribe; of one whose subdued eyes,
Albeit unused to the melting mood,
Drop tears as fast as the Arabian trees
Their medicinal gum. Set you down this,
And say besides that in Aleppo once,
Where a malignant and a turban'd Turk
Beat a Venetian and traduced the state,
I took by the throat the circumcised dog
And smote him, thus!

Stabs himself.

Lodovico. O bloody period!

Gratiano. All that's spoke is marr'd.

Othello. I kiss'd thee ere I kill'd thee: no way but this,
Killing myself, to die upon a kiss.

Falls on the bed, and dies.

Cassio. This did I fear, but thought he had no weapon,
For he was great of heart.

Lodovico. [*To Iago*] O Spartan dog,
More fell than anguish, hunger, or the sea!
Look on the tragic loading of this bed:
This is thy work. The object poisons sight;
Let it be hid. Gratiano, keep the house
And seize upon the fortunes of the Moor,
For they succeed on you. To you, lord governor.
Remains the censure of this hellish villain,
The time, the place, the torture: O, enforce it!
Myself will straight aboard, and to the state
This heavy act with heavy heart relate.

Exeunt.